THE HURDY-GURDY METHOD

by

DOREEN AND MICHAEL MUSKETT

Previously published by Muskett Music

Peacock Press

No part of this book may be reproduced in any form
without the written permission of the publisher.

Original typesetting by Michael Muskett
Diagrams by Bill Leeson
Photographs by Michael Muskett
© Doreen Muskett 1998

British Library Cataloguing in Publication Data.
A catalogue record for this book is available from the British Library

1st edition	1979	ISBN 0 946993 12 2
2nd edition. Revised and enlarged	1982	ISBN 0 946993 00 9
2nd impression	1984	
3rd edition. Revised	1998	ISBN 0 946993 07 6
French Edition. Méthode de Vielle	1985	ISBN 0 946993 01 7

ISBN 978-1-908904-98-0

Published by Peacock Press
Scout Bottom Farm,
Mytholmroyd,
Hebden Bridge
HX7 5JS

Cover illustration. Drawing by W. Dow of a 19th century French Hurdy Gurdy.
By kind permission of the German National Musuem, Nurenberg.

CONTENTS

Introduction	1
A short history of the hurdy-gurdy	3
The parts of the hurdy-gurdy	8
Strings and Tuning	10
General care of the instrument	14
Cotton and resin	15
Holding the instrument	16
The keyboard	18
How to use this method	20
Time notation	21
Pitch notation	22
Playing with the trumpette	22
Finger exercises	23
Getting around the keys	26
Playing in ¾ time	28
The wheel and the *coup de poignet*	29
The right hand and the manivelle	31
The different turns of the wheel (diagram)	33
Lesson 1 The single stroke	34
Lesson 2 The regular two-stroke	36
Lesson 3 Triple time	40
Lesson 4 The irregular two-stroke	44
Lesson 5A The first irregular three-stroke	46
Lesson 5B The second irregular three-stroke	47
Lesson 6 The regular four-stroke	48
Lesson 7 The regular three-stroke	52
The limping stroke	53
Lesson 8 The irregular four-stroke	58
Lesson 9 The six-stroke and the eight-stroke	60
Playing the key of G	62
Playing in G minor	63
Playing in C minor	64
Style and interpretation	66
How to play 18th century music on the vielle	68
Preluding	70
Ornamentation in 18th century music	71
The mediæval symphony	79
Scales and modes	83
Additional repertoire	84
The choice of an instrument	92
Buying a hurdy-gurdy	93
How to true the wheel	95
Fault finding chart	95
How to make and adjust the trompette	96
French/English glossary	98
List of original 18th century music for the vielle	99
Bibliography	100
Index of pieces	102
List of illustrations	103

Doreen Muskett

INTRODUCTION

The Genesis of The Hurdy-Gurdy Method

From 1985, Doreen and I were giving concerts in schools and elsewhere, based on the historical development of musical instruments. During our research, Doreen found a reference to an instrument no one was playing – the hurdy-gurdy. It took her fancy at once; we found an instrument and took a week's study course in France with Gaston Rivière.

Very soon people were asking for lessons and Doreen realised she needed a teaching method. We wrote this jointly, Doreen putting into the book all she had learned about technique, and working together to select the music. I also undertook all the technical aspects of producing the book. Because many of our earlier students were musically literate, the book is based upon the ability to read music and it is so laid out that players can teach themselves as they learn to play.

The second edition was reprinted a number of times pending the publication of the third edition.

Michael Muskett
June 2015

The years since the first publication of this book have seen a great change in the fortunes of the hurdy-gurdy. It is now more widely played than ever and has a following in most European countries, USA, Canada and Australia. There are many fine players and more good makers than previously.

Many aspiring players successfully make their own instruments, but learning how to play is another matter, especially for those who live far from centres of musical activity. Many people have found this book and its accompanying tape invaluable in helping them to get started.

I wrote this method for the simple reason that when I myself wished to learn to play the vielle I found that there was neither a method nor a teacher available in England. I found an instrument but there was nobody to tell me how to really make it work. For that I had to go to France.

This book is the result of many visits to France and several years of research into music and methods, old and new. I hope it will help players to avoid some of the mistakes which I made out of ignorance, and that it will help them to master, in a shorter time, the techniques which it took me several years to acquire.

This edition has been revised so as to present a more logical approach to learning, the main change being to stress the importance of learning the left hand techniques before those of the the right hand. More pieces have been introduced from the eighteenth century, which remains a largely untapped source of inspiring music.

The beginner could not do better than to follow the advice of André Dubois, whom I quote:

'Do not think that because you have a vielle on your knees, a method to guide you and a teacher to advise you, you will now be able to play. It is not as simple as that! In addition to all this, you will have to practice every day if possible, never losing courage, particularly in the early stages when tuning and adjusting the strings are so difficult. But with persistence you will get through the first stage, and the more you play and discover the delights of the vielle, in proportion to your progress your playing will give you more and more pleasure. As you become a good vielle player, try to find the opportunity to play with other good players. But I ask you, do not copy other players too much. Try to develop your own style of playing which will reflect your own personality and temperament.'

Over the years I have made many good friends among vielle players in France, and I am deeply indebted to all those who have helped and advised me: to Gaston Rivière who was my first teacher; to Armel and Marie-Noëlle Bury who helped to put me right each time they came to England; to André Dubois for the inspiration his Method gave me; to Dominique and Gilles Dubois for the joy it gave me to watch them play; and above all to Gabrielle and Hubert Marcheix for their teaching, their hospitality and their friendship. To all these, and to my husband Michael, whose help and encouragement have been immeasurable, I dedicate my method.

Doreen Muskett
March 1998

The Hurdy-gurdy Player. Oil painting by Georges de la Tour, c.1630
Note that the keyboard and arm are at right angles and that the tuning pegs are held much lower than the handle.

A SHORT HISTORY OF THE HURDY-GURDY

The hurdy-gurdy is a fascinating instrument which dates back to mediæval times, but which is today enjoying a popular revival in many countries, particularly France, both as a folk instrument and for the performance of mediæval and 18th century art music.

The hurdy-gurdy is a string instrument with a wheel (or circular bow) which sets several melody and drone strings vibrating together. The melody strings are stopped by tangents attached to sliding keys.

The familiar and rather derogatory term 'hurdy-gurdy', with its comical overtones, only came into use in the 18th century, and suggests that the instrument was not held in very high esteem in England at that time. Confusion was caused by the later use of the name 'hurdy-gurdy' for the barrel organs and street pianos of the 19th and early 20th centuries.

Other countries have bestowed more beautiful and dignified names on the instrument. The French call it *la vielle à roue* (wheel-fiddle) or simply *vielle*, while in Italy it is the *ghironda* or *lira tedesca,* in Germany, *drehleier*, and in Holland, *draailier.*

The middle ages

During the 12th and 13th centuries the hurdy-gurdy is described as either an organistrum or a symphonia. It was usually figure-of-eight shaped, and was obviously a modification of the bowed instruments of the period. These names suggest that the music played on the instrument was polyphonic, either with a continuous drone or with a melody strengthened by parallel fifths or octaves (organum).

The organistrum appears first in Spain about 1150 in stone carvings on French and Spanish churches, but notably on the portals of the cathedrals of Soria and Santiago de Compostela. It was a large, bass-sounding instrument, made for two players, one of whom turned the handle while the other used both hands to operate the keys.

This type of instrument, which would have been suitable for slow and moderately fast melodies, appeared also in England and France, but disappeared in the 13th century and was replaced by smaller instruments which were played by one musician. These could have been used to play lively melodies and dance tunes. The tangents probably acted on the melody string only, leaving the other strings as constant drones. This would be in keeping with the drone style of fiddle and rebec playing which was common at that period.

The organistrum or symphony should be seen, therefore, as an attempt to mechanise the stopping of strings and to simplify the process of bowing.

Portico de la Gloria. c.1188
Cathedral of Santiago de Compostela

In the 13th and 14th centuries, in addition to the more usual figure-of-eight or guitar-shaped symphonia, small rectangular, box-like symphonies are depicted, with a row of keys along either the top or bottom edge.

We cannot know for certain what mechanism lay under their protective lids (and some mediaeval artists themselves seem to have been ignorant as to how they worked), but it was almost certainly the same as we know it to have been for the last four hundred years. It was common practice for mediæval artists and stone masons to copy each other's designs and in this way mistakes were perpetuated, such as continuing the row of keys along the entire length of the box of the symphony, a concept which would not work in practice as it leaves no space for the wheel, which in this instrument is concealed by the lid.

Another unworkable idea which has been perpetuated in almost every book and article on the organistrum is that it had rotating tangents which turned like door keys to act on all three strings together. This idea originated from a faulty drawing published by Martin Gerbert in the 18th century in his 'De Cantu' and which is said to have been a copy of an illustration in the 13th century Codex of St Blasien (since destroyed by fire). Several modern makers have attempted to reconstruct an organistrum with rotating tangents, but have found that this system does not work, and have instead used the normal sliding keys and tangents with perfect success.

I have one of these instruments myself which I have used in many concerts and recordings, and which sounds wonderful (see page 78).The keys can be pushed up from below or lifted from above, which is slower, and both these methods of playing can be seen in 12th century Spanish carvings. This may explain why scholars thought that there were two different mechanisms.

There were also two variants of the hurdy-gurdy. One was an instrument with a wheel and a crank but no keys or tangents, the melody string being stopped by the fingers, as on a violin. The other had keys and tangents, but the strings were bowed. An instrument of the second type is still being made and played today in Sweden, where it is called the *nyckelharpe*.

The organistrum or symphonia was often shown in pictures being played by angels or by King David, and must have been an important instrument for church music, judging by this quotation from Robert Mannyng (c.1303).

> 'Yn harpe, in thabour, and in symphan gle,
> Wurschepe God, yn troumpes and sautre,
> Yn cordys, on organes and bellis ryngyng,
> Yn all these, wurschepe ye hevene kyng.'

Miniature from the Luttrell Psalter (c.1330) showing a symphony being held the wrong way round
Compare with the illustration on page 79

The symphony was also one of the instruments which an accomplished minstrel was expected to play, according to the 'conseils aux Jongleur' written by Guiraut de Calanson in 1210. The jongleur had to play the pipe-and-tabor, the citole, the symphony, the mandore, the monochord, the rote, the harp, the gigue and the psaltery.

The Renaissance
During the period between the 14th and 16th centuries music underwent great changes. With the growth and development of harmony with its vertical chord sequences, the inflexible symphony with its constant drone found itself obsolete, and it has no place in the art music of the renaissance. Writers at that time refer to it as a beggar's instrument. Marin Mersenne, in his 'Harmonie Universelle' (1636) has this to say about the symphony, before going on to give a detailed description of it:

Old Sarah, the hurdy-gurdy player. From Mayhew's 'London Labour and the London Poor' (1851)

> 'If gentlemen of quality normally played the Symphonie, which we call the "Vielle", it would not be so despised as it is, but since it is played only by poor people, and particularly the blind who earn a living with this instrument, it is less highly esteemed than others which do not give as much pleasure. But I will nevertheless explain this instrument, for knowledge is no more the property of the rich than of the poor, and there is nothing so base or so lowly, in nature or in art, that is not worthy of consideration.'

Shepherd and shepherdess, porcelain figures
Collection Michele Fromenteau

The eighteenth century
Although it seems that professional musicians in the seventeenth century did not use the hurdy-gurdy, clearly it never ceased to enjoy great popularity among folk musicians and peasants. It is often shown in pictures together with bagpipes, an instrument often associated with shepherds. Thus it became one of the fashionable instruments taken up by the aristocracy at the courts of Louis XIV and XV during the vogue for pastoral entertainments and *fêtes champêtres*, and composers once more turned their attention to it.

During the seventeenth and the first half of the eighteenth centuries, the vielle underwent refinements and improvements, and its compass was increased to two octaves. Two forms were popular, the *vielle-en-guitare*, and the *vielle-en-luth*, with the lute-shaped vielle gradually ousting the guitar shape, and many beautifully decorated instruments were made for wealthy amateur players.

An enormous amount of music was written at this time for the vielle and for the musette (a sweet-toned bellows-blown bagpipe), by such composers as Boismortier, Buterne, Chédeville, Hotteterre, Corrette and Baton.

Several methods were published, the best and most thorough being those of Baptiste Dupuit (1741) and François Bouin (1761). In both of these the technique of using the *coup-de-poignet* or *trompette* is described in detail.

The *trompette* is a device used for articulating the notes by means of a buzzing bridge. The earliest definite appearance of the trompette on a hurdy-gurdy is in the painting by Hieronymous Bosch (c.1450-1516) of the Garden of Earthly Delights. It is also shown clearly in pictures by de la Tour (1593-1652) and Callot (c.1622), but it is not mentioned by Praetorious (1620) or by Mersenne (1636), who both give detailed drawings and descriptions of the vielle.

One might be forgiven for thinking that because the wheel simplifies the bowing and the keys simplify the stopping of the strings, the hurdy-gurdy presents no difficulties to the performer. On the contrary, the vielle players have exploited the techniques of the instrument to the limit of its capabilities and the virtuoso players have acquired skills no less brilliant than those required for any other instrument. The eighteenth century *Principes* by Dupuit devotes a large section to the techniques of playing expressively and in the correct style.

After the French revolution the *vielle* in France again retired to the relative obscurity of the countryside, where the brilliant style of playing, which was developed in the eighteenth century has been carried on in an unbroken tradition to the present day, especially in the Berry, Bourbonnais, Auvergne and Limousin regions, where it is used for fast bourrées, walzes and other regional dances. Many beautiful nineteenth century instruments are still being played, and *vielle* makers today can scarcely keep up with the demand for new instruments.

In no other country has the hurdy-gurdy been as important as it has been in France. However, it is still to be found in Spain, Hungary and Ukraine. Until the nineteenth century it was also popular in Bohemia, Slovakia and Romania, but it is no longer heard in these countries although many interesting instruments can be seen in the museum in Prague.

As far as England is concerned, the picture is rather confusing, but it seems unlikely that the hurdy-gurdy was ever as widely used as it was on the continent. Undoubtedly, it was seen and heard from time to time during the 18th and 19th centuries, but with the notable exception of the blind street musician

'Fanchon la Vielleuse', heroine of many popular plays, ballets and operas in the 18th and 19th centuries

Members of the folklore group, l'Eicolo dau Barbichet (Limoges)

"Old Sarah", who played in London during the first half of the 19th century*, the musicians seem to have been mainly poor Savoyards, often mere children, who travelled throughout Europe with their *vielles*, peep-shows, and marmottes. Their instruments were likely to have been in bad repair, or with strings missing, and this might help to account for the low esteem in which the hurdy-gurdy was held by English musicians. The following verse from the highly popular comic opera 'Fanchon la Vielleuse', illustrates the sad plight of these young Savoyards.

> Aux montagnes de la Savoie,
> Je naquis de pauvres parents;
> Voilà qu'à Paris on m'envoie,
> Car nous étions beaucoup d'enfants.
> Je n'apportais, hélas! en France,
> Que mes chansons, quinze ans,
>   ma vielle et l'espérance.

> In the mountains of Savoy
> I was born to poor parents;
> So I was sent to Paris,
> For we were many children.
> And so aged fifteen years, alas,
> I took with me to France,
> Only my songs, my hurdy-gurdy,
>   and my hopes.

In Britain today there is growing interest in playing the *vielle* and a number of makers are now producing fine instruments. A school of playing and regular study courses have been established.

In Spain the hurdy-gurdy is found today in two regions, Asturia and Galicia, but it was seldom heard except at special festivals and processions, particularly at Christmas and Easter.

In Germany the *leier* was frequently heard until the 19th century as a popular instrument for dance music, and Schubert was moved to write his tragically beautiful song "Der Leiermann", after hearing a wandering beggar musician. Today a thriving new school of makers and players has grown up in Germany, centred on Frankfurt.

In Hungary until recently the hurdy-gurdy was still played by a few old men in the Szentes region. Here too, young makers and players are bringing back to life the old songs and dances of the unique Hungarian style of playing—a style very different from that of any other country—which, thanks to the recordings and transcriptions made by Béla Bartók early this century, was saved for posterity.

* Mayhew. London Labour and the London Poor. Vol.III. 1851

1997 edition

Today there are many players, especially in the UK and Germany. France is no longer the fount of all knowledge, but retains importance as the originator and keeper of the 19th century playing tradition. Although France and French players still set the standards to be measured by, the hurdy-gurdy is played around the globe from Finland to Australia and California, which is a major centre in the USA with many players and bands.

The Hurdy-gurdy Society has done much to foster interest and put people in touch with each other. In Holland and Spain, too, there are Hurdy-gurdy Societies and a new interest, both in their traditional styles and in the French style.

NB The Hurdy-gurdy Society no longer exists.

The Hungarian hurdy-gurdy player, Robert Mandel

A NEW DEFINITION

The hurdy-gurdy is a musical instrument with melody and drone strings, a keyboard and a circular bow. A loose bridge, known as the trompette, gives a rhythmic buzz controlled by the wheel and is used for dance music.

It has two names according to the music being played, vielle for chamber music and hurdy-gurdy for popular dance music.

"Hurdy" because it is supported on the thighs (hurdies [Scot.]) and "gurdy" because it is held in place with a strap or belt, (from gird – to fasten or secure with a belt).

THE PARTS OF THE HURDY-GURDY
in English and in French

1 Head	1 La tête
2 Tuning peg	2 La cheville
3 Movable nut	3 Le sillet
4 Lid of keybox	4 La cache-clavier
5 Tangents	5 Les sauteraux
6 2nd chanter	6 La 2ème chanterelle
7 Trompette	7 La trompette
8 Wheel	8 La roue
9 Trompette bridge, dog	9 Le chien
10 Fly	10 La mouche
11 Crank	11 La manivelle
12 Ear	12 L'oreille
13 Key	13 La touche
14 Sympathetic strings	14 Les timbres de résonance
15 Small drone	15 Le petit bourdon
16 Large drone	16 Le gros bourdon
17 Oil hole	17 Le trou à graissage
18 1st chanter	18 La 1ère chanterelle
19 Bridge	19 Le chevalet
20 Peg for adjusting trompette	20 La cheville pour règlage du trompillon
21 Cord for adjusting trompette	21 Le tirant
22 Tail-piece	22 La cordier
23 Knob	23 La poignée

THE PARTS OF THE HURDY-GURDY

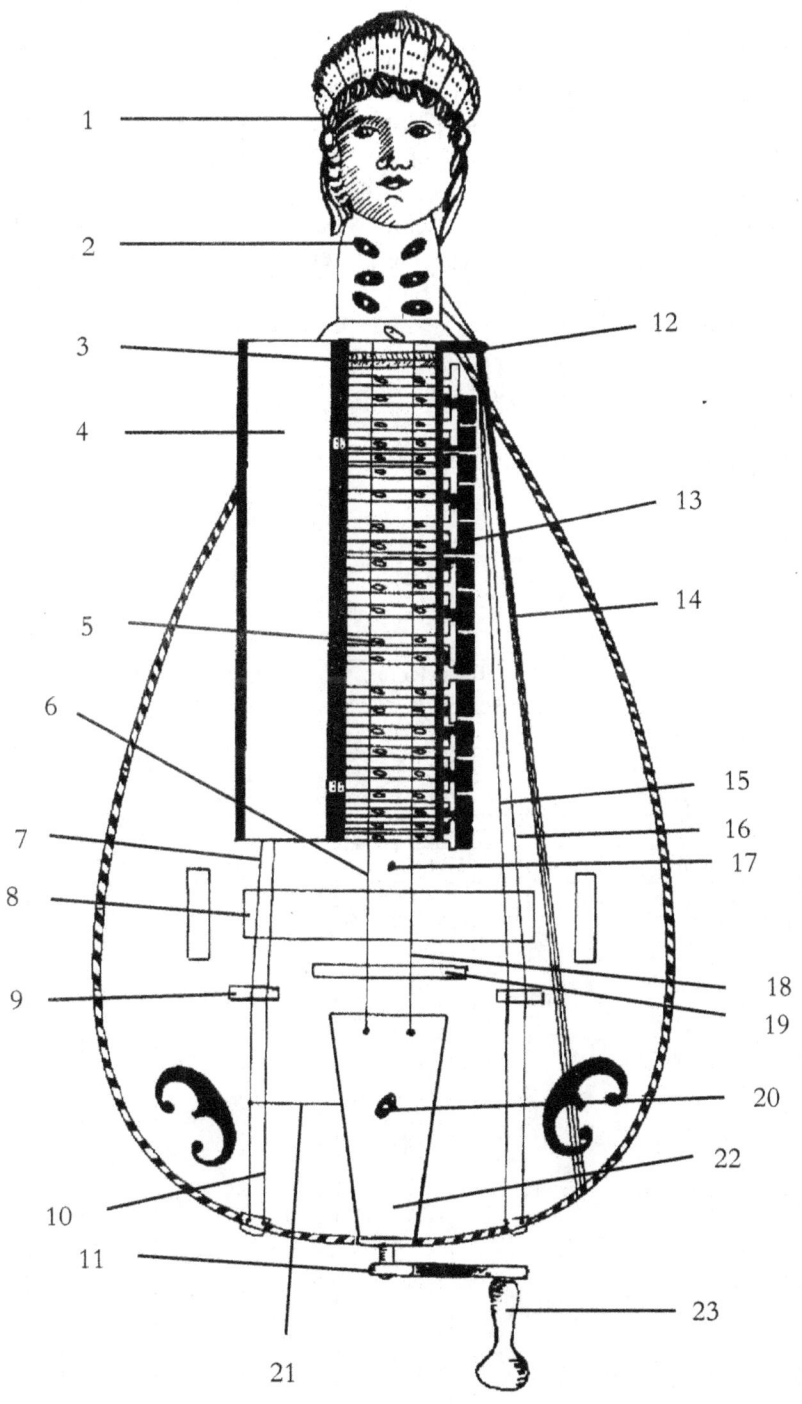

STRINGS AND TUNING

The hurdy-gurdy has six strings and sometimes four sympathetic strings in addition. For their names and positions see pages 11 and 12.

Plain gut strings are used for the chanterelles, mouche and trompette, silver or copper wound on gut for the bass drone strings, and steel for the sympathetic strings. Violin and violoncello strings are used for modern instruments, according to the charts below, but thinner strings may be needed on the smaller instruments of the eighteenth and nineteenth centuries. For instance, 5th and 6th bass viol strings may be tried in place of the 'cello strings for the bass drones.

Instruments vary in their requirements and you should experiment with strings of slightly varying thickness until you achieve the tone quality and balance which you find agreeable.

Nowadays specialist suppliers can offer strings of different weights and characteristics. Nylon strings are not recommended.

As the pegs are quite hard to turn it is usual to use a wooden tuning key.

THE SYMPATHETIC STRINGS
(*timbres de résonance*)

These are thin metal strings (usually four in number) which lie near the *gros bourdon* (bass drone) string, a few millimetres above the soundboard. The strings are tuned with a small metal key or with violin E string tuners.

The metal strings hold their pitch much better than the gut strings and serve as a standard pitch to which the melody strings may be tuned. When the melody string reaches the right pitch the sympathetic strings resonate, thus confirming that the correct pitch has been achieved. The sympathetic strings should be regularly tuned using a standard such as a pitch pipe.

The strings are commonly tuned to g^1, g^1, c^1, c^1.

THE G-C TUNING

Name of string	String used	Diameter in thousandths "/mm	C tuning	D tuning
Chanterelles	Violin D	38/0.969	g'	g'
Trompette	Violin D or 'cello A	40/1.02	c'	d'
Mouche	Violin D	43/1.08	g	g
Petit bourdon	'cello G	51/1.28	c	-
Gros bourdon	'cello C	72/1.82	-	G
Sympathetic strings	Guitar or banjo B		c' c' g' g'	

HOW TO TUNE THE STRINGS

G-C tuning (open string G)

The diagrams on the right show the two tunings most often found today. Although the D tuning is becoming more popular, the principal tuning used in the 18th century is still the one most widely used, namely the G-C tuning, so-called because one can play in the keys of G (major and minor) and C (major and minor).

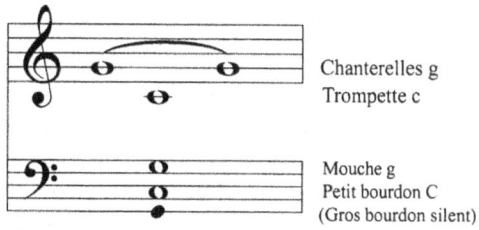

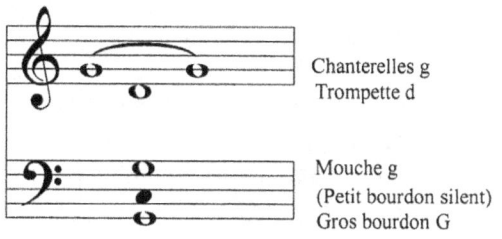

Most modern instruments have a hitch for the melody strings, so that they may be silenced at will. The bridges over which the drone strings pass have two notches for each string, so that any string may be silenced by disengaging it from the wheel. Either the *petit bourdon* is used, or the *gros bourdon*, according to the key, the other being hitched back.

When one changes from the key of C to the key of G it is necessary to tune the *trompette* up one tone and also to re-adjust it. Some instruments are fitted with a device which enables the pitch to be changed without altering the tension of the string, so that the *trompette* does not need re-adjusting.

Tuning the strings

Disengage all the strings except the first *chanterelle*. Turn the wheel steadily and fairly fast with the right hand while turning the tuning peg by means of the tuning key or *tourne-à-gauche*. See that all the strings are wound onto the pegs in the same direction, so that you turn them to the left (anti-clockwise) to raise the pitch.

The *chanterelle* is tuned to the first G above middle C on the piano. A pitch pipe or tuning fork may be used to give the right note. If the hurdy-gurdy has sympathetic strings, these should be tuned first and the *chanterelle*s can be tuned to them.

Engage the second *chanterelle* and bring it to the same pitch as the first. Two strings which are almost, but not quite, in unison will give a steady rapid beat or pulse which becomes gradually slower and then disappears as the two notes are brought into unison. The ability to hear these beats will improve with practice.

The *trompette* can now be tuned to the C a fifth below the *chanterelle*s. You can test it by pressing the third black key, which gives C an octave higher.

The *mouche* (fly) is tuned next, to the G an octave below the *chanterelle*s.

Finally the *petit bourdon* is tuned to the C an octave below the *trompette*.

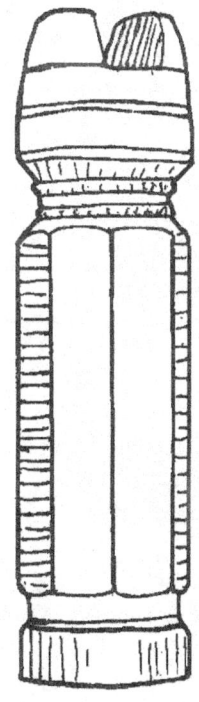

TIP
When fitting new strings make sure that they tighten as you turn the tuning peg anti-clockwise (to the left).

Tourne-à-gauche or wooden tuning key

The D Tuning

This tuning is used in the Berry and Bourbonnais regions and it is the tuning given in the two modern French *vielle* methods by Rivière and Dubois.

It was first advocated by Charles Baton in his 'Memoir on the Vielle in D' written in 1752. He put forward three advantages for it, namely, that the tone is improved, that it goes better with the flute and the violin and other instruments, and that it is more suitable for accompanying the voice. The pitch range is wider than on the *vielle* tuned in G-C because the first chanterelle is tuned an octave higher than the second, and the gros bourdon is a fourth lower than in the other tuning. (Of course, this does not mean to say that one can play any more notes on a *vielle* tuned in this way.) Evidently, his suggestions were ignored by other composers of the century.

The drones are kept the same whether one is playing in the key of G or the key of D. Most players do not use the *mouche*.

You will find that some tunes sound better in the C-G tuning and others in the D-G tuning.

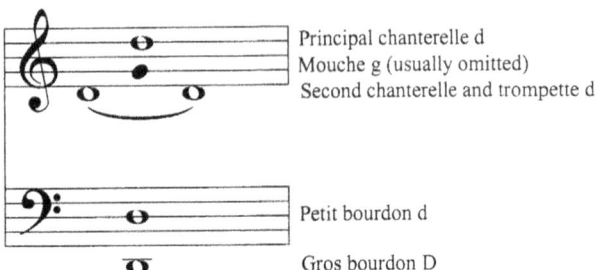

Principal chanterelle d
Mouche g (usually omitted)
Second chanterelle and trompette d

Petit bourdon d
Gros bourdon D

Name of string	String used	Diameter in thousandths "/mm	D/G tuning
1st Chanterelle	Violin A	27/0.68	d"
2nd Chanterelle	Violin D	38/0.96	d'
Trompette	Violin D or 'cello A	40/1.02	d'
Mouche	Violin D	40/1.02	g (usually omitted)
Petit bourdon	'cello G	51/1.28	d
Gros bourdon	'cello C	72/1.82	D
Sympathetic strings	Guitar B		d' d' d' d'

TUNING THE INTERVALS OF THE SCALE

The scale of the hurdy-gurdy is determined by the points at which the tangents touch the strings. For perfect intonation it is essential to check the position of each tangent regularly. To check the first row of tangents, disengage all the strings except the first chanterelle. Start with the most important interval, which is the octave from the open G to the G above (7th black key). This octave must be perfect when the tangent is at right angles to the string. If the octave is not perfect, it must be corrected by adjusting the nut. The nut should be a tight fit, but should not be glued.

If the upper G is sharp, move the nut towards the bridge. If it is flat move the nut away from the bridge.

It is easier to hear if this octave is in tune if you also engage the *mouche*, which sounds the G one octave below the chanterelle, but take great care that this octave is very accurately tuned before testing the second G of the chanterelle.

You cannot check the absolute pitch of a hurdy-gurdy string by plucking, as this gives a different pitch from the note sounded by the wheel. Always turn the wheel briskly and not too slowly when tuning.

Now test the position of each of the other tangents in turn, adjusting them when necessary until the scale is in tune. If at first you cannot do this by ear, you may use a piano or electronic pitch meter.

If, having done this, you find that many of the tangents are touching the string at a sharp angle away from the wheel, then the nut needs to be moved towards the bridge. Conversely, if many of the tangents are turned towards the wheel the nut should be moved further from the bridge, so that as many of the tangents as possible are straight, as this makes for a better tone and a more even touch to the keys.

To adjust the second row of tangents, engage the second chanterelle and tune the open strings perfectly in unison. Turn the wheel and play each note, one by one, up the scale, adjusting the tangents in the second row where necessary, to give a perfectly smooth sound. This must be done by ear and not by eye, because the two tangents will not always be at the same angle when they are in tune, owing to variations in the quality of the strings or in the position of the nut. Note that these adjustments are harder to make if the instrument is not fitted with a separate nut for each of the two chanterelles.

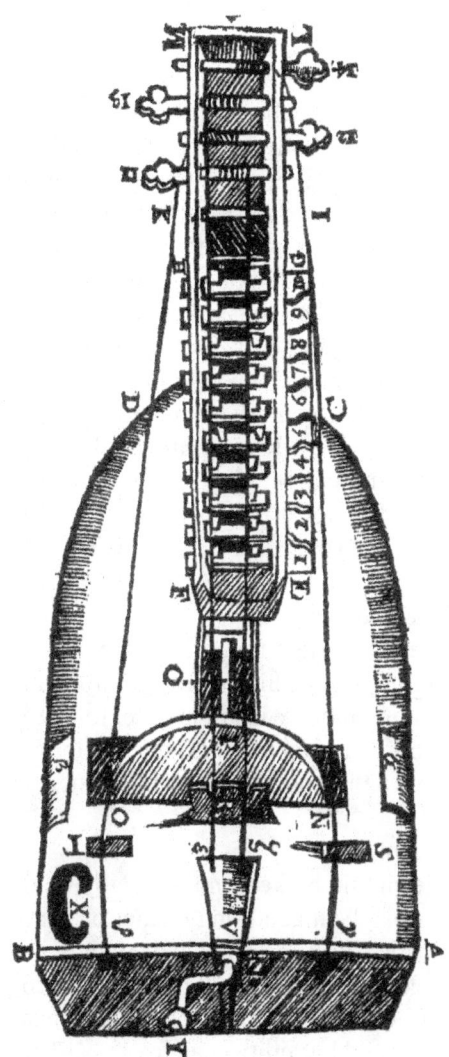

Technical illustration showing the working parts of the hurdy-gurdy. Marin Mersenne (1636)

GENERAL CARE OF THE INSTRUMENT

Avoid all extremes of temperature and keep the *vielle* in a dry place, but not near a source of heat. In humid weather, or with changes of temperature, the wood moves, and the wheel may lose its perfectly round shape, which is indispensable for the smooth continuity of the sound.

Avoid touching the wheel with the fingers as this may make it greasy and cause gaps in the sound. If you should inadvertently touch the wheel (or if an onlooker should) you can repair the damage by treating the area with a little powdered resin.

Oiling

From time to time the axle should be oiled, introducing the oil through the special hole between the keybox and the wheel, and also where the axle protrudes from the body. Use a feather from which all the barbs have been removed except at the very tip.

You should ascertain whether your instrument has wooden, brass or steel bearings, for on this will determine your choice of oil. For metal bearings you should use mineral oil, but sparingly, since the acids in the oil will attack the wood. For this reason you must never use mineral oil on wooden bearings, such as are fitted to 19th century instruments. For the latter you should use fine olive or almond oil, or castor oil diluted with turpentine.

Important: Do not allow any oil to get onto the wheel! One drop could have dire results.

The Wheel Cover

This serves to protect the wheel from dust, damp, sunlight or inquisitive fingers. But it may be removed during playing if one wishes, in order to increase the sonority. For convenience it is attached by means of a thin cord to the bridge of the bass drone.

The Case or Box

The vielle should be kept in a specially made case. Soft cases can be made using leather or upholstery-grade plastic, quilted or padded, with a lining of woollen cloth. (Wool and silk have better properties than synthetic materials for insulating against temperature and humidity changes.)

Hard fitted cases protect the instrument better. Rectangular boxes are strong but bulky and heavy; they have plenty of space for compartments for spare strings, cotton, resin, oil, *tourne-à-gauche*, etc. Moulded or shaped cases of wood or fibreglass are the best, though more difficult to make.

Putting cotton on the chanterelle

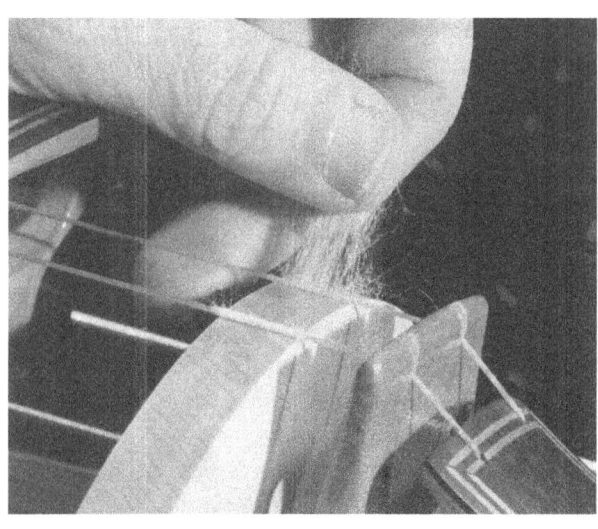

Cotton

You need to wind the cotton onto the strings at the point of friction with the wheel. There are two reasons for this. Firstly to prevent the strings from wearing, and secondly to stabilise the tone and make it less harsh.

Use very fine cotton-wool with long filaments and no impurities or lumps. One puts less cotton on the chanterelles than on the other strings. Too much, or not enough, will spoil the tone, or cause the notes to sound out of tune. First prepare the string by rubbing a little resin onto it to help the cotton to adhere.

To apply the cotton, when you have chosen a tiny piece you must pull it out and divide the filaments evenly until it is the same width as the wheel and about the thickness of a spider's web. Lift the string off the wheel with the second finger of the left hand and slip the cotton carefully between the string and the wheel.

Then, while turning the wheel evenly and slowly with the right hand, wind the cotton onto the string, twisting and rolling the string between the thumb and forefinger. If it is wound on well the cotton should not slide along the string. After renewing the cotton, a little resin should be applied to the wheel.

It is important to examine the cotton on the strings each time you play your hurdy-gurdy, to make sure that it has not worn away, particularly on the chanterelles where they pass over the right edge of the wheel.

Resin

Resin is used on the wheel for the same reason that violinists use it on the hair of their bow. It creates the friction necessary to set the strings vibrating, and is best applied little and often.

Take care never to touch the surface of the wheel with a finger tip, as this will deposit a small amount of grease on the wheel, causing a gap in the sound as the wheel revolves.

Use a good quality violin or 'cello resin on the hurdy-gurdy wheel and avoid using too much. Hold the block of resin against the wheel and give it no more than one or two turns. Powdered resin can also be used and applied with a small piece of velvet. It is sometimes kept in a hollowed out section of the *tourne à gauche*. Apply powdered resin to the wheel between the chanterelles and the petit bourdon, so that in case any bits are not completely powdered, they will be caught up in the cotton of the trompettes or mouche, and not in that of the chanterelles.

Do not allow excess resin to accumulate on the soundboard. Use a fine brush or duster to clean it.

Michael Muskett demonstrating the correct sitting position for playing the hurdy-gurdy

HOLDING THE INSTRUMENT

Seated

The vielle is held on the lap, attached firmly by a strap around the waist, so that it does not move about while being played. The belt must be adjusted so that it is really tight. A broad leather strap is the best, made so that the length is adjustable. This fits onto the single button below the carved head, and on the right it is fastened to the nearest of the two buttons at the tail end.

Sit upright on a hard chair, such as a dining chair, well balanced, with the feet apart and firmly on the floor, the left foot a little further forward than the right, and so that the head of the instrument is lower than the handle end. Take care not to droop over the instrument.

The instrument should be tipped slightly away from the body, so that the keys fall back easily when they are released.

Hold the left arm away from the body so that the hand is free to slide along the top of the keybox. The left hand should be in line with the arm.

The right arm is held slightly out from the body, so that the shoulder, elbow and wrist are in a line, as the hand holds the knob of the *manivelle*, with the palm facing towards the instrument.

Standing

For playing while standing or walking in a procession, a second strap is used. This is attached on the left to the same button as the first strap, passing up under the left arm, across the back, down over the right shoulder, and then it is threaded between the soundboard and the tailpiece, and is then attached to the furthest of the two buttons at the tail end near the bass drones. It should be about 1.7 metres long.

The French hurdy-gurdy player, Gaston Rivière
Note the shoulder strap and positions of the hands

Waist strap

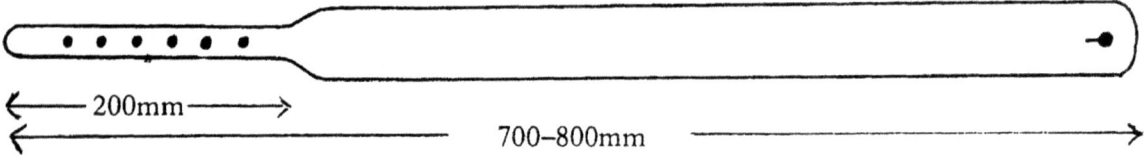

Holding the hurdy-gurdy in your lap, measure round your waist from the left to the right buttons before ordering a strap.

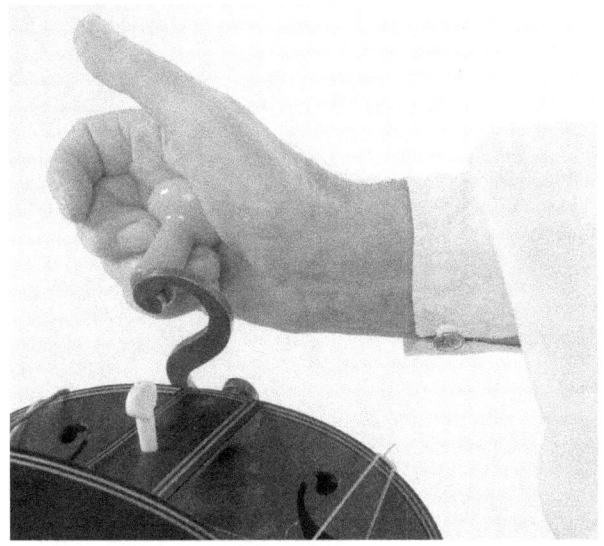

The right hand holding the manivelle

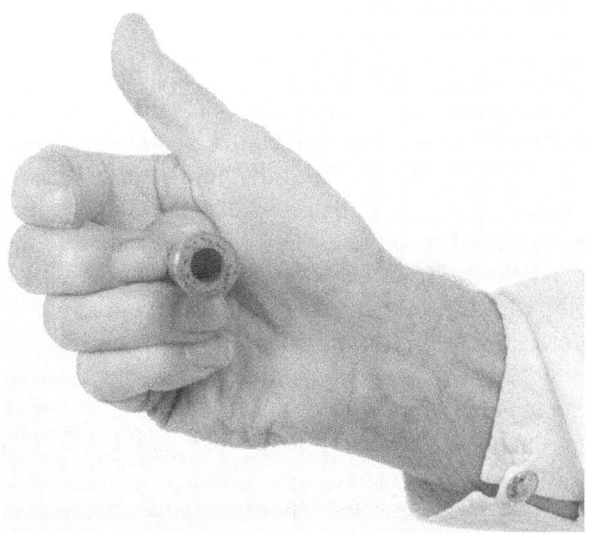

The right hand showing the position of the knob (poignée)

The Right Hand
Hold the knob with the palm of the hand facing inwards towards the instrument and not downwards towards the floor. The little finger and third finger curl into the palm, while the thumb rests on the top of the knob (*poignée*), and together with the other two fingers it forms a kind of cage within which the knob is able to move freely. This will be more fully explained later on.

The Left Hand
The four fingers of the left hand are used, but not the thumb. The fingers are numbered 1 to 4, starting with the index finger.

The hand is slightly cupped so that the palm is in the air and the left edge of the hand and the ball of the thumb rest lightly on the lid of the keybox, so that the hand can slide easily along it.

The fingers should be curved round to reach the keys with the first joint. Do not lift the fingers further from the keys than necessary, as this would hamper their speedy return during fast passages. Always try to keep the ends of the fingers at right angles to the keybox. The thumb should be held away from the first finger.

The pressure on the key must be firm enough to produce a clean and steady sound, but do not press the key so hard as to distort the strings as this makes the note go sharp. More experienced players can learn to control the finger pressure to produce a vibrato, a technique which is especially effective in slow airs.

Position of The Left Hand on the keybox

THE KEYBOARD

The arrangement of the keys on the hurdy-gurdy is similar to that on a piano or harpsichord, with black keys for the naturals, and white keys for the sharps and flats. But the action of the hurdy-gurdy keys is quite different from that of either the piano or the harpsichord. It most closely resembles that of the clavichord, in that the key carries a tangent which stops the melody string at a precise point, which determines its vibrating length and therefore its pitch. Also, as long as the finger depresses the key, the tangent remains in contact with the string, thus producing a sustained note as long as the wheel is turning.

Most hurdy-gurdies have two tangents fixed to each key, so that two melody strings can be played in unison (see Fig. 6, page 19). The keys fit into slots or mortices, one on each side of the keybox (see Fig. 9, page 19). In the playing position the instrument is tipped forwards so that the tangents rest about 4mm below the strings. The finger pushes the key upwards until the tangents touch the strings firmly, and on being released, the key drops back to its original position because of gravity, the string sounding its open note, G, again.

As the touch-pieces of the keys are situated on the far side of the keybox, it is not possible to see them while playing, but one can easily see which keys one is touching by looking at their points of exit. At rest they are flush with the keybox, but in use they stand out about 10mm.

One should familiarise oneself with the key pattern and corresponding notes (see diagram below), but aim to play by touch as soon as possible, rather than looking down at the keys. In the top octave the keys are so close together that there is no room in the bottom row for an F key. When necessary the tangent of the F natural may be turned to the right to give F sharp.

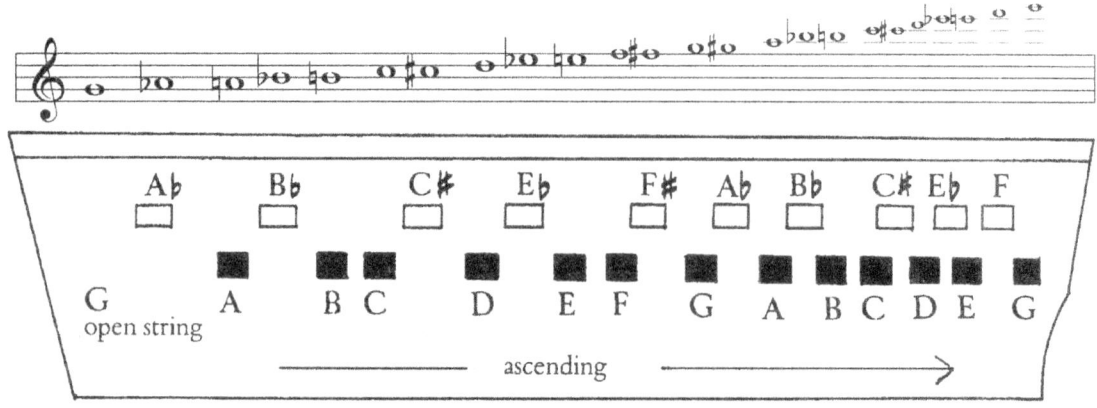

Near side of keybox as seen by the player

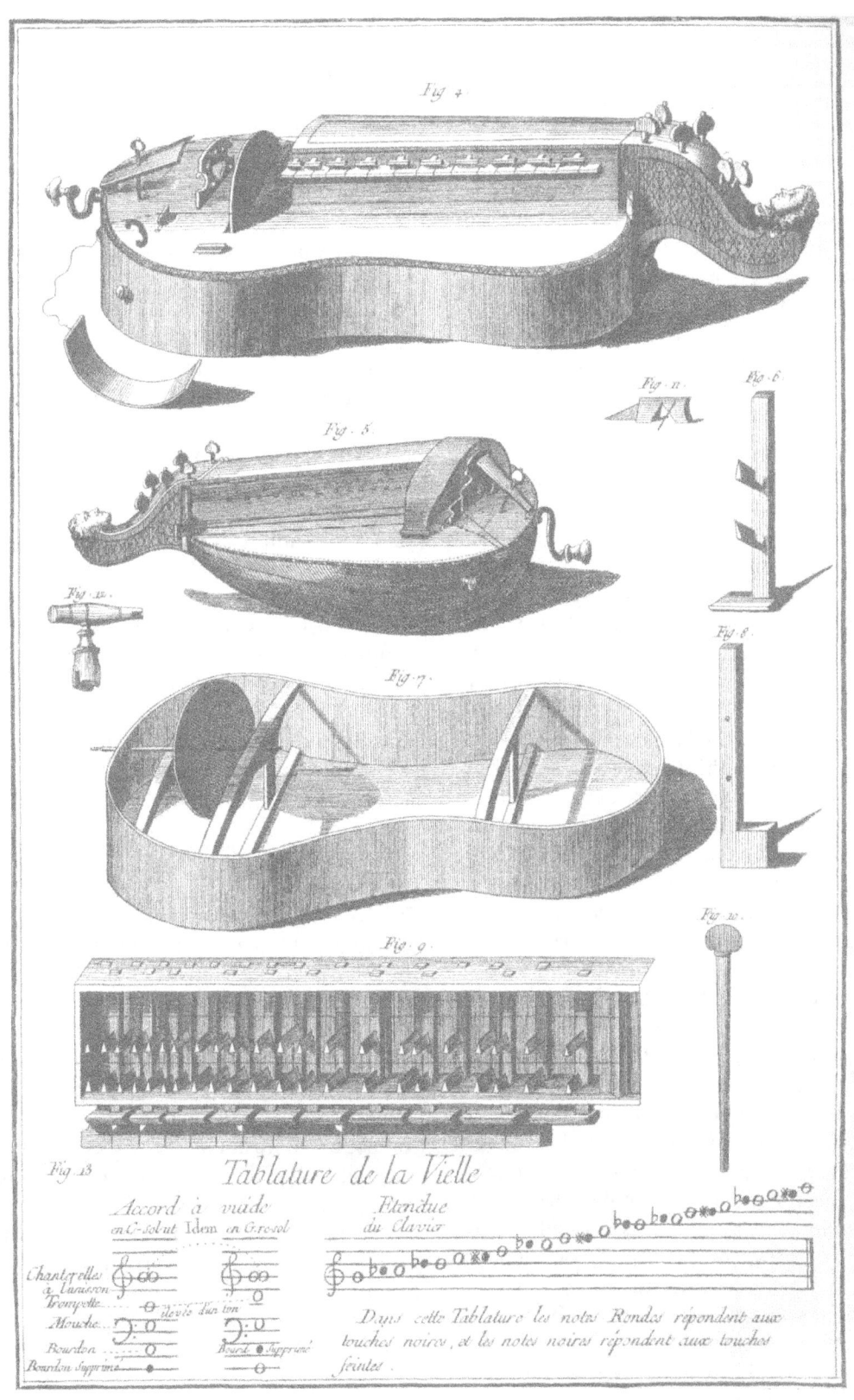

A group of instruments which are sounded by means of a wheel
From the *Encyclopédie* of Diderot and d'Alembert, Paris (1767)

HOW TO USE THIS METHOD

This book will help you to learn the basics of playing the hurdy-gurdy. Music notation has to be used since this is how the concepts of time and pitch are shown. It goes without saying that those who can read music will find the book of more value than those who can not. If you are one of the latter you will learn to read music as you go along.

Playing an instrument means developing a set of techniques. There are two stages to this. The first is to understand clearly what you are aiming to do and the second is to develop methods for achieving it.

Practice
Work through the book progressively, mastering each exercise as well as possible before proceeding to the next, because they have been carefully graded.

Basic work should be undertaken with the crotchet (1/4 note) at 60-80 beats per minute. Use a metronome if you have one. Only when you can play the task in hand reliably and keeping a steady pulse (be it a tune, exercise or rhythmic pattern) should you speed up, little by little, attempting to keep the same accuracy as you do so.

Do not try to perfect a whole piece at once. Practise short sections and repeat them non-stop. Take a four bar phrase, or even a group of four notes, and repeat them until the fingers are under control, then join the sections. If you avoid making errors the passage will begin to run freely and the difficulty will melt away.

It cannot be too strongly stressed that the way to make secure progress is through *slow practice*. In addition, all playing should be *strictly in time*. Slow practice may seem tedious but it lays the foundation for a reliable technique and is quicker in the long run. You may find this discipline hard to follow but it is the true road to solid progress.

Furthermore, much quicker progress is made if you play regularly, even if not for long. It is better to practise little and often than to have days without playing and then binge. Music is unlike other forms of study. Comprehension alone is not sufficient; physical skills and responses have to be developed.

Study the right and left hands separately
The development of technique is in two parts; the left hand and the right hand. Although much is made of the trompette, it is not this which produces the melody. This is the function of the left hand, which controls pitch and rhythm. It follows that in the early stages of learning it is more important to develop a sound left hand technique than to spend excessive time on the right hand. This refinement will come later.

The left hand
Practise the left hand on its own while turning the wheel steadily without applying the trompette (hitch the string). It helps to say either the pitch names or the finger numbers while you play, especially if you do not read music fluently. Silent left hand practice is also helpful (i.e. without the wheel).

The right hand
Once you feel secure with the left hand you can begin work with the trompette. Play very simple rhythmic shapes at first, then find one of the tunes or exercises you can already play, decide which notes you are going to articulate or mark with the trompette, and practise this rhythmic pattern using the open string and trompette only. (You may hum the melody meantime, or count the beats aloud.) When this is under control set a slow tempo (70-80 beats per minute) and play both hands together. Take great care to synchronise the two hands and not to add the trompette inadvertently, e.g. do not play two crotchets when a minim is indicated.

Not all pieces are enhanced by using the trompette and slow melodies are seldom improved by its use. The trompette comes into its own to enhance the rhythm in vigorous pieces, such as marches and dance tunes.

The trompette
The wrist is not flexed in playing, but rather transmits the force of the arm to the manivelle. Because the trompette is so characteristic of the hurdy-gurdy there is a tendency to spend time and effort developing this technique before laying down the foundations of a technique which will enable you to play a simple tune. Tunes are, in any case, very often effective without it. Always learn to play a piece without the trompette before adding it. The trompette is not an essential part of the music, but does lend definition and rhythmic force.

It is not an easy technique to master on your own and it is important that you are shown how to do this by a good player.

TIME NOTATION

Time notation is represented by notes of different colour or shape. The basic pulse of most music is walking speed, whether it be faster or slower. This pulse is normally represented by crotchets (1/4 notes). Notes lasting two beats or steps are represented by a white note, the minim, while two notes to a beat are represented by a pair of quavers (1/8th notes).

If you find it difficult on your own to get to grips with notation it is advisable to take a few lessons with someone who can read music (using your singing voice or any other instrument) and study one of the books on theory. Do not be put off by the word 'theory'; it is merely a codification of what is done in practice.

Symbol	American terms	English terms	Number of turns
♬	Sixteenth note	Semi-quaver	¼
♪	Eighth note	Quaver	½
♩	Quarter note	Crotchet	1
♩	Half note	Minim	2
o	Whole note	Semi-breve	4

Time signature	Beats per bar
2/4	♩ ♩
4/4	♩ ♩ ♩ ♩
3/4	♩ ♩ ♩
3/8	♫ ♪
6/8	♫♫ ♫♫

The notes are not of equal strength. In common time (4/4) for instance, there is a stronger pulse every 4th note and this stronger note is shown by placing a vertical line in front of it. This is known as the bar line and the space within two bar lines is known as the bar (measure). The first note in the bar is always the strongest and should be slightly stressed, either by making it fractionally louder or by dwelling on it.

Clap or tap each row of notes while counting aloud. Then tap one row with the left hand and another with the right hand simultaneously.

Using a metronome

Working with a metronome may help if you have difficulty with time. This will not be easy at first, but patience will be rewarded by the acquisition of the firm rhythmic control which is the mark of a good player.

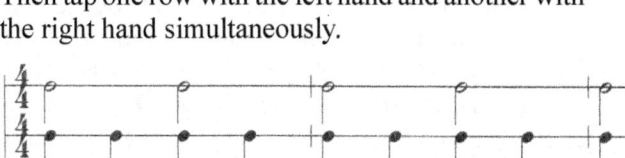

PITCH NOTATION

Pitch notation is shown by placing the notes on a set of five lines known as the stave. Notes are placed both on the lines and in the spaces, and each line or space represents one pitch or one key to touch. These pitches are set by the curly shape at the beginning of each stave. This is merely an ornate letter G and curls around the second line up, indicating that this line is called G. From this the other pitches may be worked out. It is easy to remember that the names of the second, third and fourth spaces ascending spell the word ACE, and your key-note, C, is always in the third space.

The first three notes on leger lines above the stave also spell ACE.

PLAYING WITHOUT THE TROMPETTE

Disengage the trompette string and use only the melody strings and the low G drone for all the pieces in this section.

Note that the four fingers of the left hand are used, but not the thumb, and they are numbered 1 to 4, starting with the index finger. With no fingers down the open string G is sounded.

Rest the left hand on the lid of the keybox. The outer edge of the left hand and the base of the thumb should be in contact with the lid, but not the palm, which should be slightly cupped.

Turn the manivelle evenly and fairly fast, about once a second, to produce a good tone while counting aloud, '*one*, two, three, four, *one*, two, three, four...', repeating this several times without stopping the wheel, and *giving one revolution for each count*. Each turn should start with the knob at the top, in line with the main bridge and tailpiece.

Signs used in this method
The left hand.
Written below the notes
0 = open string
1 = 1st finger
2 = 2nd finger
3 = 3rd finger
4 = 4th finger

Left hand exercises
Before going on to discuss the right hand technique using the *trompette,* let us first look at some of the difficulties of the left hand, which are often neglected. It is important to develop good fingering habits, which are essential for a fluent technique and for good phrasing. It is a good idea to do some daily practice of finger exercises, scales and broken chords.

The correct pressure of finger and key can be determined by listening. If the tangent touches the string too lightly or comes against it too slowly or tentatively the vibrating string will rattle against it. If the pressure is too great the string will be stretched, causing the note to go up in pitch. A firm, decisive touch is needed.

Remember to keep the manivelle turning steadily and in time with the fingers. Also check your sitting position and the angle of the instrument with the photographs on pages 7, 15, 16 and 68.

FINGER EXERCISES

Exercise 1
With the 4th finger, touch the first black key, 'A', and release it again, repeating the movement many times regularly and firmly while turning the wheel steadily.

 = 1 turn

𝅗𝅥 = 2 turns

𝅝 = 4 turns

𝄇 Repeat sign

Exercise 2
Do the same, using the 3rd finger on the second black key, 'B'.

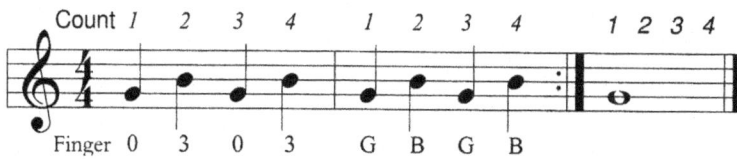

TIP
At first you may find it easier to turn the right hand in free time.
Later, you can co-ordinate the two hands.

Exercises 3, 4, 5
Similarly, use each finger in turn, and give even turns of the wheel for each note.

Exercise 6
In this exercise you use each finger in turn, giving one turn of the wheel for each note.

Exercise 7
Notes lasting two beats (minims) are given two turns of the wheel.

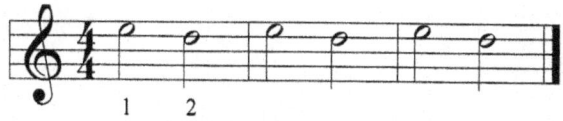

Exercise 8
Notes lasting four beats (semi-breves) are given four turns of the wheel.

FINGER ARTICULATION
Repeated notes on the same degree

Exercise 1

If you are not using the trompette you must articulate repeated notes by releasing the key briefly, so that the open string sounds momentarily between the note and its repetition. (Later we will use the *coup de poignet* to articulate repeated notes while keeping the key down, but these exercises are to be played with the trompette string disengaged.) The wheel may be turned freely at first.

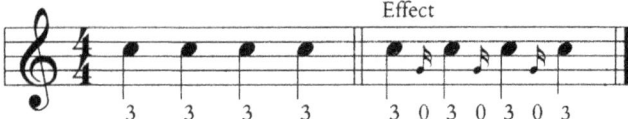

Exercise 2

We also frequently need to make use of repeated notes in order to change the finger position, and this must be done as neatly as possible, trying this time to avoid sounding the open string. The next two exercises are for changing various fingers on the same note.
Give one turn for each crotchet.

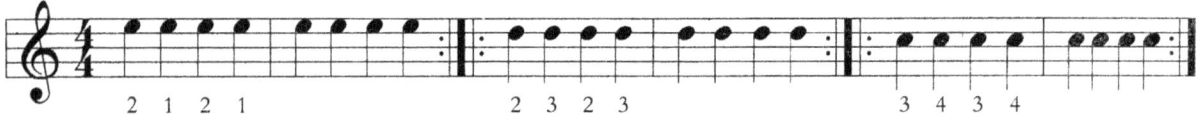

STACCATO and LEGATO

Notes with dots over them are played very short.

Notes under an umbrella or slur are played smoothly joined.

Notes under one slur must be separated from notes under another slur, by shortening the last note in each phrase, whether they are in two's, three's or longer phrases.

Fingering can be used to shape the melody by articulation. Good fingering can help you, while bad fingering can ruin the phrasing, as shown in the next two examples in which the same notes are given different phrasings. In a) the fingering forces you to separate the two phrases, while in b) it enables you to play all the notes legato.

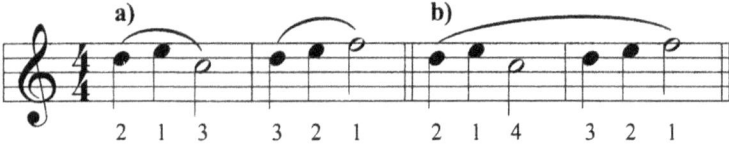

These pieces are in the key of C major, in which there are no sharps or flats. The C key is the third black key from the left.

Engage the low C drone, but disengage the trompette string for these exercises.

Play these pieces without the trompette, turning the manivelle in free time at first, and then with one turn for each beat.

Fingering b) is better than a).

Synchronised turning of the wheel

When you have mastered the left hand the next stage, before actually using the trompette, is to control the wheel speed so that you are making one turn for each crotchet (¼ note) beat, synchronising the downbeat with the start of each note in every bar.

AU CLAIR DE LA LUNE

VENDÔME

Organistrum players. Drawn from a miniature
in the Hunterian Psalter (12th century)

GETTING AROUND THE KEYS
The principles of fingering

The fingering used in playing a piece of music affects both the ease of playing and the musical effect. You move up and down the keyboard by changing the hand position and these changes must be done in sympathy with the musical phrases.

There are six ways of changing position.
1) By a simple shift.
2) By using repeated notes.
3) By temporary extension.
4) By simple extension.
5) By contraction.
6) The whole hand shift.

1) The simple shift
This is used when moving by step (e.g. to the next note).
Examples a) and b) are good, but c) is less good. Do not wait for the four fingers to be used up before changing position.

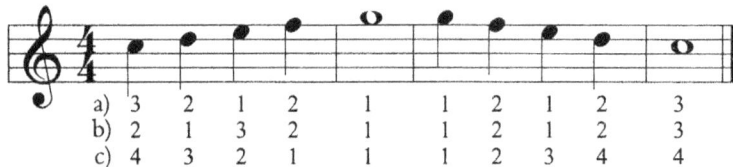

2) Using repeated notes

3) Temporary extension
Extension of one finger, the others remaining in their first position.

4) Simple extension
Extension of one finger, the other fingers taking up a new position.

5) Contraction

Leave out one finger and use the next finger in its place, the other fingers taking up new positions.

LULLABYE

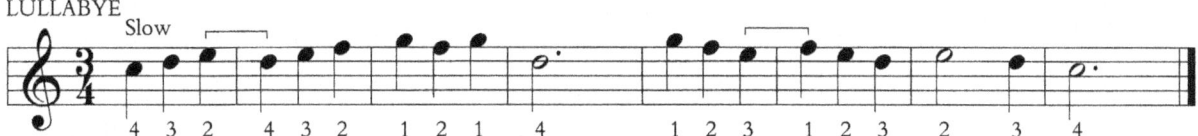

6) The whole hand shift

When the range of the melody is greater than four notes, as for instance in going up the scale of C, the whole hand must be moved up in order to play the rest of the scale. Move the forearm with the hand, taking care not to twist the wrist in order to accommodate the new position.

Notes within one bracket are played without shifting position.

SCALE FINGERINGS   BROKEN

C major

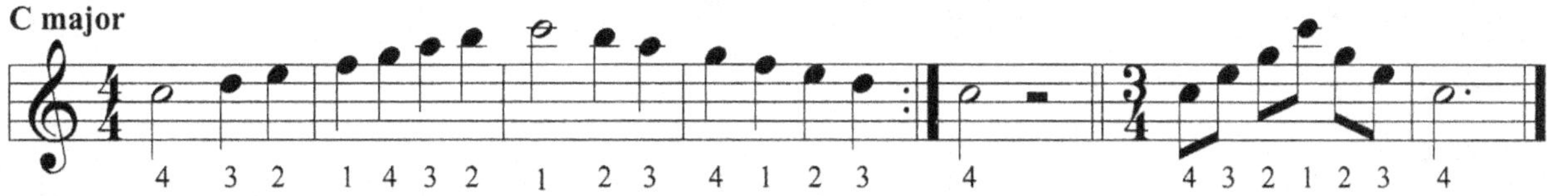

C minor

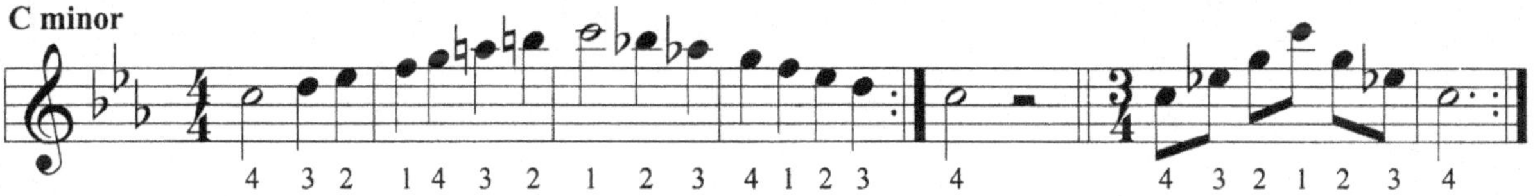

G major

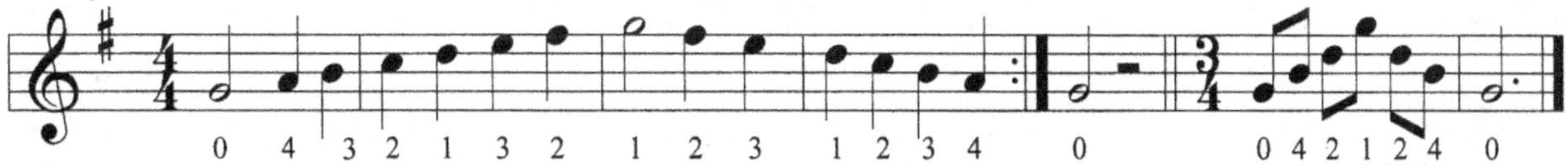

G minor

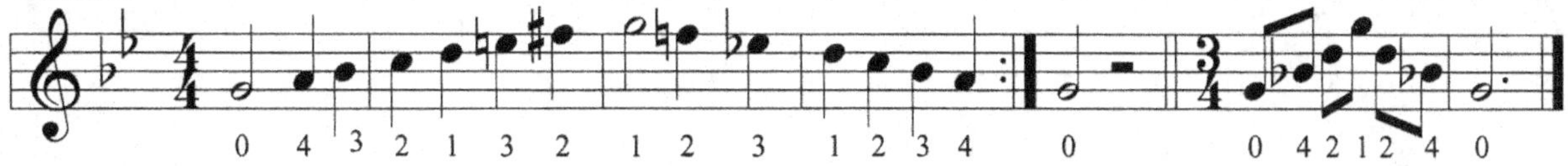

Chromatic scale

PLAYING IN 3/4 TIME

Turn the manivelle steadily as before, but this time count **1**, 2, 3, **1**, 2, 3, giving one turn for each crotchet count, two turns for each minim and three turn for each dotted minim.

THE WHEEL AND THE *COUP DE POIGNET* OR *TROMPETTE*

"The wheel is to the vielle what the bow is to the violin. It is the wheel which gives the instrument its soul and its diversity. It is the wheel which determines the character of a piece and which distinguishes one phrase or part from another by the different turns given for that purpose; it is this which one calls the *coup de poignet*. Without the aid of the wheel the vielle would not shine or stand out."

Thus wrote François Bouin in 1761, and no one who has heard an expert vielle player today would disagree with his words. Although there are different styles of playing, and many pieces are effective without the use of the *coup de poignet*, yet the trompette string gives the instrument a completely different character - more brilliant and exciting, and it would be foolish not to make full use of its possibilities.

In order to understand the use of the *coup de poignet* it may be helpful to compare it to the up-strokes and down-strokes of a violinist's bow; to separate the notes he must change the direction or increase the speed of the bow. With the wheel as a continuous bow, the *détaché* or attack is achieved by giving the wheel a momentary extra impetus, which causes the trompette bridge to beat on the soundboard, causing the typical buzz. Why call it the *'coup de poignet'*? Because, while the fingers encircling the knob are fairly relaxed, and the arm moves freely at the shoulder and elbow, it is the *wrist* which is firm (though supple), and through which the force is transmitted to the thumb for the downward *coups* and to the third finger for the upward *coups*.

The *coups* or strokes of the wheel must be very precise, clear-cut and sharply defined. How many *coups* one makes in each bar of the music depends partly on the character of the music as well as on the taste of the performer.

Usually, for gay, lively tunes, one uses the *coup de poignet* to accent each note, but in tender or gentle pieces it is not necessary to mark every note. One may play a group of eight quavers, for example, without marking each quaver on every quarter turn of the wheel, but only the first note of the group. But one must mark any repeated notes, Gs on the open string, and from time to time mark the longer notes, or the first of a group of quavers.

The terms *coup de poignet* and *trompette* are interchangeable.

Instruments which produce a continuous sound, such as the hurdy-gurdy and the bagpipes, have a problem when it comes to articulating notes. The piper does it by using grace notes; the hurdy-gurdy player uses the trompette.

The trompette is a loose bridge (*chien*) over which the string passes, and which is balanced in such a way that a slight acceleration of the wheel causes it to beat rapidly against the soundboard, producing a buzzing sound.

Each instrument must have its *chien,* or dog, specially fitted, and each player has his own ideas as to how this should be done and what type of response and quality of tone he requires. Obviously, for playing 18th century chamber music in a drawing-room you would not use the same trompette that you would use to play for outdoor dancing.

If you learn to make your own *chien* you can, with time and patience, achieve your own ideal.

See pages 96 and 97 for details of how to make and adjust the trompette bridge.

FRENCH LESSON
Coup de poignet
pronounced *coot pwa'nyay*
Coup [ku], knock, blow, tap, nudge or stroke.
  Un coup de baton; a blow with a stick
  Un coup de froid; a cold snap
  Un coup de dents; a bite
  Un coup de chance; a stroke of luck
  Un coup de sifflet; a whistle (and the name of a restaurant)
  Un coup d'état; a sudden overthrowing of the government and seizure of power by others
  Essayer un coup; to have a try
Le poignet, wrist. *Faire quelque chose à la force du poignet*: to do something by sheer strength of arm.
La poignée, knob

The trompette adjusting string (the *tirant*) should wrap around its peg so that the peg turns to the right (clockwise) to tighten it. The string should leave the peg at its tip so that the *tirant* is parallel with the soundboard. The *trompette* string should be pulled only slightly out of line and certainly no more than its own thickness. If the string gives a grating tone the *chien* is too short.

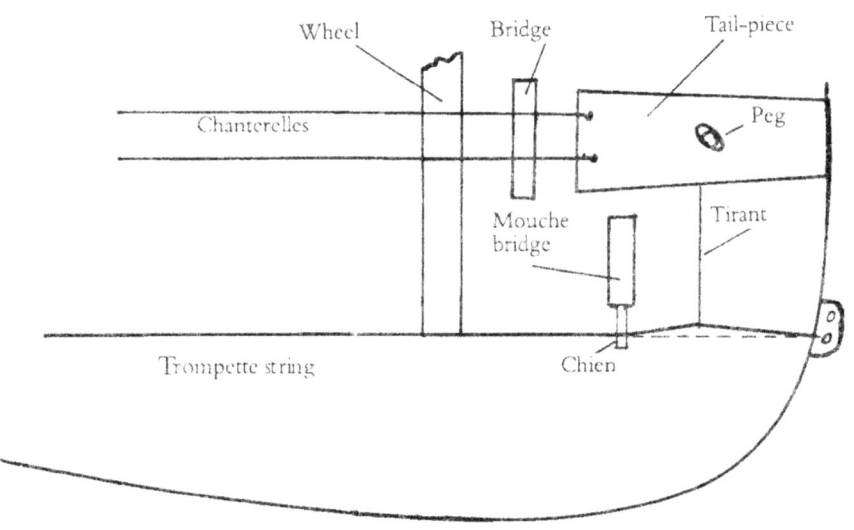

Correct position of the wrist

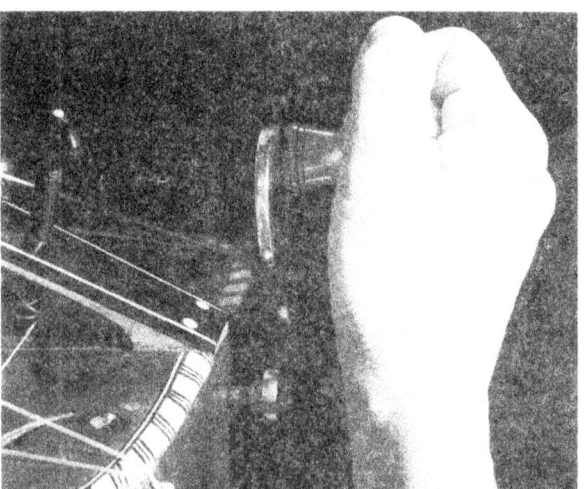

Faulty position of the wrist.

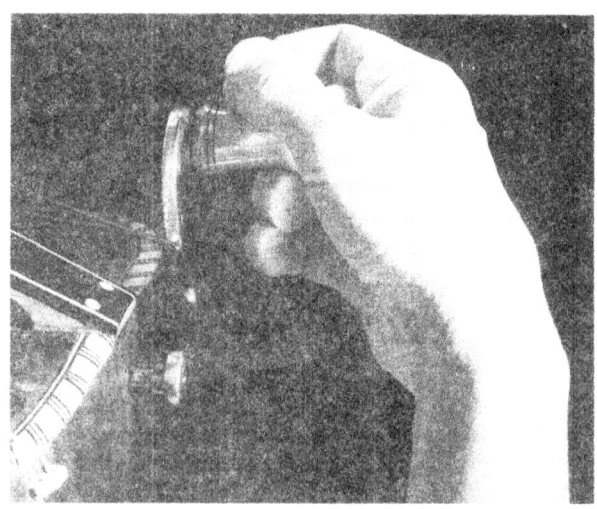

THE RIGHT HAND AND THE MANIVELLE OR KNOB

Hold the knob with the palm of the hand facing inwards towards the instrument and not down towards the floor. Do not drop the hand, but flex it upwards, bending at the wrist. Keep the elbow down. The little finger and third finger curl into the palm, while the thumb rests on top of the knob (*poignée*), and together with the other two fingers they form a kind of cage within which the knob is able to move freely.

This freedom is an indispensable condition for acquiring the *détaché*, which is the articulation given by the *coups de poignet*. The knob butts against its cage according to the various positions of the *manivelle* during the extremely rapid series of strokes which make up the *détaché*. Avoid grasping the knob tightly.

Neither big movements nor great force are needed to make the *trompette* buzz. Control is only achieved by giving light, vivacious strokes, which are arrested almost at the same instant and yet make up a continuous circular movement.

Some players find that they do not have enough control over the wheel unless they hold the knob firmly all the time, whilst others seem to let it go almost completely each time it goes round, as they open the fingers just before the down-stroke.

Note that the down and up-strokes will not be in a vertical plane, but slightly oblique owing to the angle at which the hurdy-gurdy is held.

The word *poignée*, meaning knob, should not be confused with *poignet* - the wrist.

There are four areas of the hand which convey the force to the knob when one performs the *détaché* or articulation:

1) The base of the thumb.
2) The first joint of the thumb.
3) The tips of the first and second fingers.
4) The side of the ring finger.

Take care not to make the mistake of flexing the wrist in the vertical plane, following the wheel round by dropping the hand. The fist should be kept up. In more advanced playing the same rule largely holds, but the wrist is supple and free to rotate slightly.

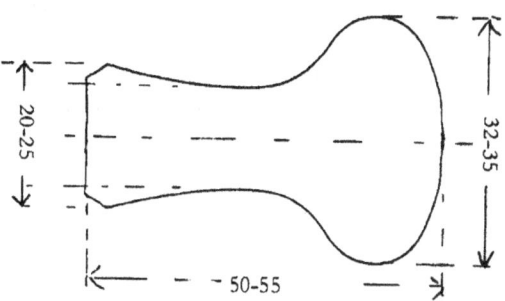

Average dimensions of the knob in mm

The profile of the knob and its dimensions are important, and it should be made of fine-grained wood, ivory or porcelain. The knob should spin freely on its axle

ON LEARNING THE STROKES OF THE WHEEL

In order to learn the *coups de poignet*, or different strokes of the wheel, it is necessary to practice them every day "diligently, patiently and incessantly"*, starting with the simpler ones and gradually progressing to the more difficult ones, slowly at first and later on increasing the speed.

It is assumed that the beginner will have an instrument which has been well set up and regulated by the teacher, so that the *trompette* speaks clearly, accurately and easily. Without this the following exercises would be useless. But in any case, the player is advised to read the detailed instructions given on pages 96 and 97 on how to make and adjust the trompette bridge, and in the absence of a teacher, should listen to our accompanying cassette, so as to have the right sound in mind.

When practising the exercises one does not need more than two strings, a *chanterelle* and the *trompette*. After tuning these strings, adjust the little peg in the tail-piece (the *tirant*, which pulls on the trompette string), by turning it to the left for a stronger buzz, and to the right for a weaker sound, and as this will change the pitch of the string slightly, it may be necessary to tune it again.

* Method by Bouin, 1761.

Nigel Eaton

Vielle player from the Auvergne adjusting his trompette while entertaining passers-by in the Place du Trocadero, Paris

THE DIFFERENT TURNS OF THE WHEEL
AND THEIR APPLICATION

THE WHOLE TURN	THE REGULAR 2-STROKE	THE FIRST IRREGULAR 2-STROKE
2 3 2 3 4, 4 4, 8	2 3 2 3 2, 4 4, 8	2 2 2 4
THE SECOND IRREGULAR 2-STROKE	THE FIRST IRREGULAR 3-STROKE	THE SECOND IRREGULAR 3-STROKE
2 3 3 4 2, 4 8, 8	2 3 2 3 2, 4 4, 8	2 3 2 3 2, 4 4, 8
THE REGULAR 4-STROKE	THE REGULAR 3-STROKE	THE IRREGULAR 4-STROKE
2 3 2 3 2, 4 4, 8	6 9 12 8 8 8	2 3 4, 8

33

LESSON 1
The single stroke
Le coup de un

Before you start you must adjust the trompette string so that the chien gives a fine, delicate and continuous buzz when you turn the wheel at about one turn per second. Now turn the wheel at a speed just below this, so that, while the trompette is now silent, yet the slightest nudge or acceleration will make it sound.

Then, according to the speed at which you wish to play, you may adjust the trompette to respond at a higher speed or at a lower one.

Use *chanterelle(s)* and *trompette* only. Starting with the knob at the top, give a short, sharp, downward stroke with the base of the thumb and continue to turn the wheel smoothly until the knob returns to the point of departure, when you repeat the stroke. The buzz of the trompette should be heard for the shortest possible moment at the beginning of the stroke, and for the remaining turn of the wheel only the G of the trompette string sounds, without any further buzz.

Keep the arm relaxed but not loose and take care not to jerk, and do not twist or bend the wrist.

Repeat exercises 1a), 1b) and 1c) many times over until you can control the buzz and the glide for the three note values.

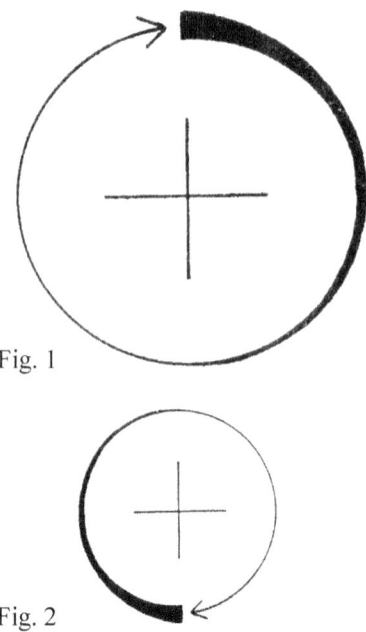

Fig. 1

Fig. 2

In order to develop an even technique, practise also starting at the bottom. Give the wheel a slight impetus with the tip of the 2nd finger on the stroke as you pull back your arm.

You should establish the tail-piece as the starting point and return there at the end of each stroke.

Exercise 1

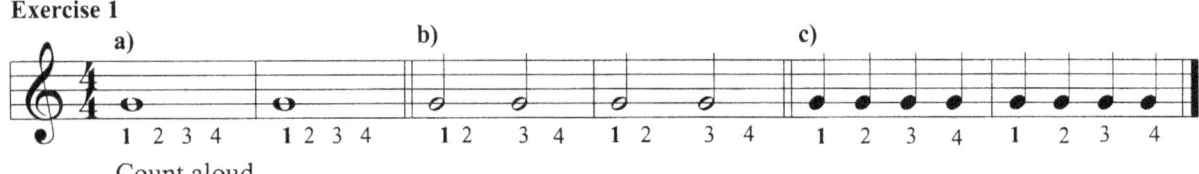

Count aloud

At first it may be necessary to stop at the top in order to check the position of the knob each time. Afterwards try to turn the wheel continuously, without interrupting the glide of the wheel, but giving the coup or stroke once on each rotation, at a speed of about one turn a second.

TIP!
Place a large mirror on your right so that you can observe your hand position.

Exercise 2

SIGNS USED IN THIS METHOD
Right hand. *Written above the notes*
↓ Down-stroke
↑ Up-stroke
o Whole turn

Now synchronise the left and right hands.
The beat should not be faster than a moderate walking pace.

This tune may also be played with finger articulation
and no trompette.

Exercise 5
Make two turns of the wheel for each minim, *but be
careful not to give more than one stroke or buzz at
the beginning of the first turn*, and to go round gently
the second time, or the effect will be the same as for
two crotchets.

> **Before proceeding to Lesson 2 repeat
> the Preliminary Exercises and Tunes on
> pages 23-28 with the trompette, using the
> single stroke for crotchets.**

LESSON 2
The regular two-stroke
Le coup de deux

There are two equal strokes. Starting with the knob at the top, give the first stroke downwards and the second stroke upwards, with the third finger.

Exercise 1

Right hand only

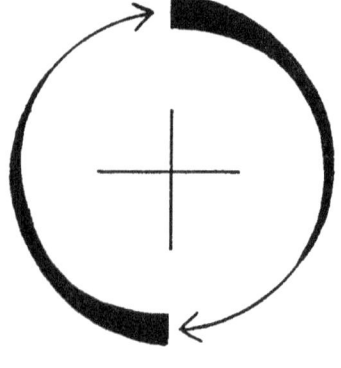

Reminder

The following symbols are used to indicate the coups de poignet

↓ down-stroke
↑ up-stroke
　 whole turn

TIP
It is helpful also to practise this stroke starting at the bottom (6 o'clock).

Exercise 2

Play two quavers for each turn of the wheel

When a note has to be repeated more than once, as in the Buffoon's Dance you can keep the finger down while the repeated note is accented only by the *coup de poignet*, but it will sound clearer if a separate finger stroke is given for each note.

In a passage like the following, it may be helpful also to change fingers on the repeated notes, depending on the tempo.

Exercise 3

TIP
Take any of these bars as a repeated exercise, either as a melody or on one note only.

Exercise 4

36

VAUDEVILLE

SAVEZ-VOUS PLANTER LES CHOUX?

In 2/4 or 4/4 time we use the following turns of the wheel

Note value	Turns of the wheel
♪	½ turn
♩	1 turn
𝅗𝅥	2 turns

When you have mastered these three note values you will be able to play a tune such as The Buffoon's Dance. Practise the rhythm first on one note with the trompette and then try the tune.

TIP
First learn to play the tune reliably without the trompette.

Exercise 5
The Buffoon's Dance -
Trompette rhythm only

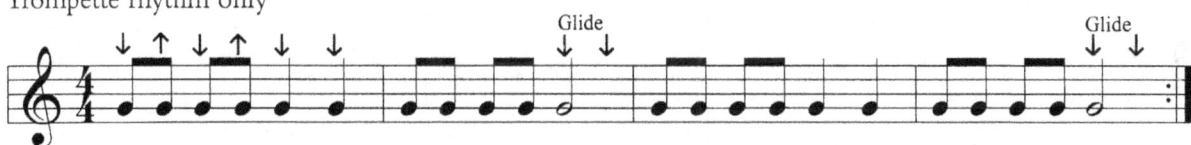

THE BUFFOONS' DANCE

Arbeau. 16th century

37

GO TELL AUNT RHODIE

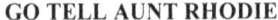

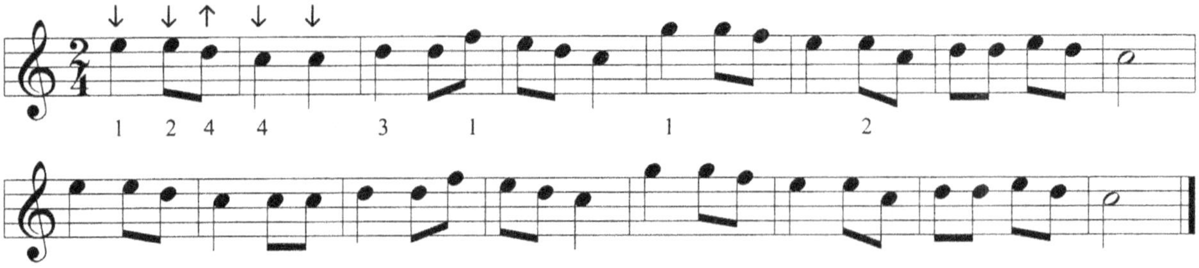

BOBBY SHAFTO

Lively

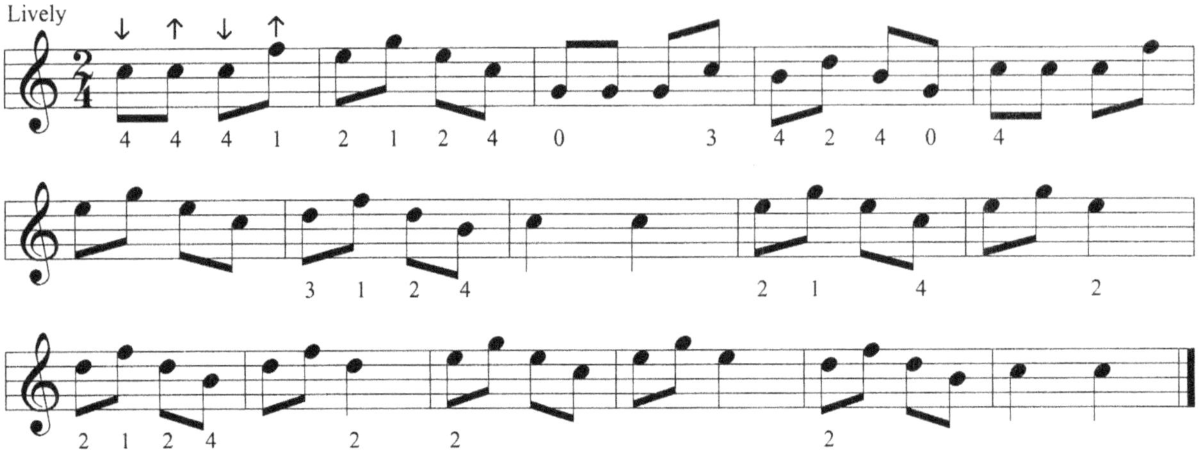

SIMPLE GIFTS American Shaker melody

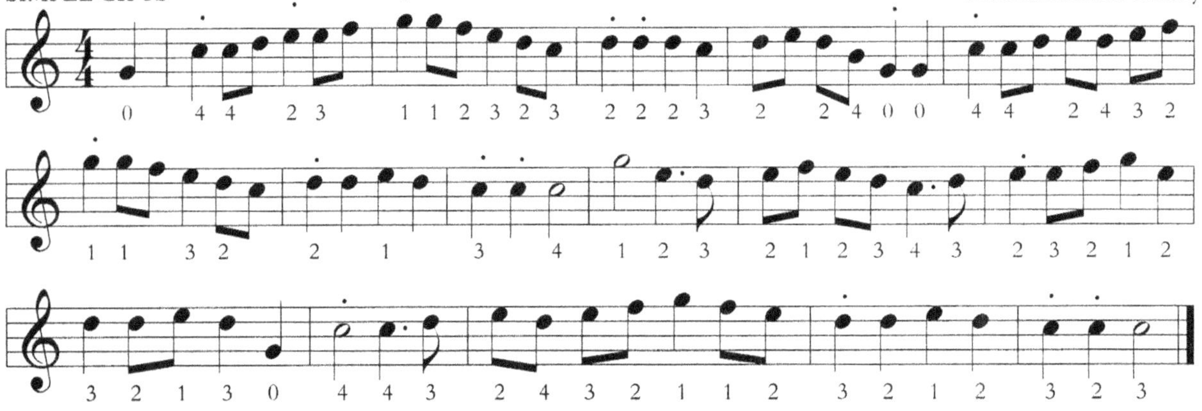

QUITTEZ PASTEURS (Les Pistolets)

French. 18th century

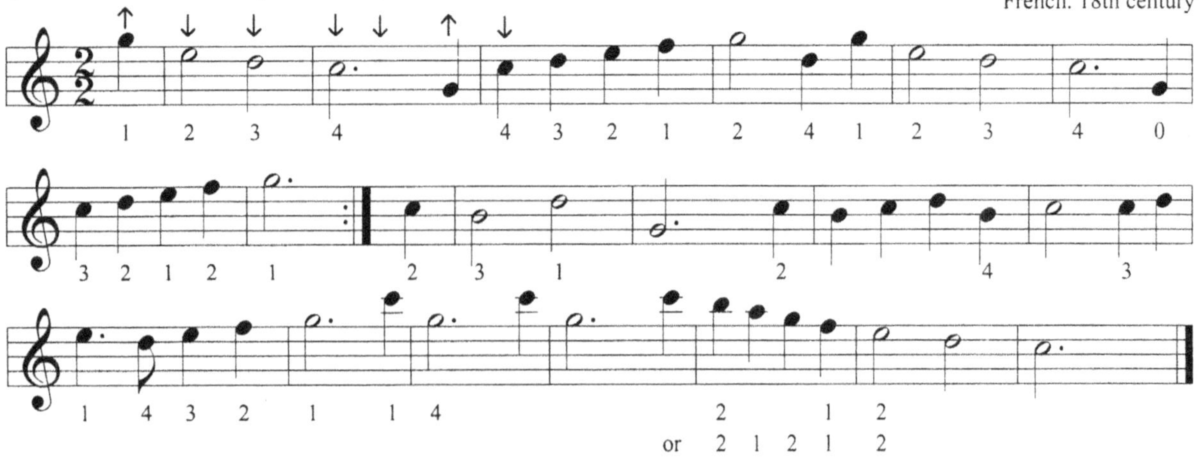

KIEKBUSCH

LA POLKA DU PÉE FAULON (Simplified)

Fish following a boat, attracted by the sound of a symphony
From a miniature in an English Bestiary (14th C.)

LESSON 3
Triple time
Mesure à trois temps

There are two distinct ways of playing in triple time, depending on whether the music is slow or fast. If the music is slow you use the single stroke as in Lesson 1.

Slow triple time
If the time signature is 3/4 and there are many groups of four semi-quavers, e.g. the first Prelude by Bouin on page 67, use the turns as shown in the table on the right.
Each bar will begin with a downstroke.

Similarly, if the time signature is 3/4, the music is marked "slow", and there are many ornaments and trills, as in Reveillez vous, one gives the same turns.

Both the following tunes should be played with one turn per crotchet but they may sound better without the trompette accent.

Note value	Turns of the wheel
♪	½ turn
♩	1 turn
𝅗𝅥	2 turns
𝅗𝅥.	3 turns

REVEILLEZ VOUS

First collection. Chédeville l'Aîné

See page 71 for an explanation of the ornaments.
See also Lamento di Tristano, page 81.

DRINK TO ME ONLY

Quick triple time

Halve the turns of the wheel.
See page 42 for diagrams.

Give half a turn for each crotchet. This means that if the first bar begins with a down-stroke, the second bar will begin with an upstroke, the third with a downstroke, the 4th up, and so on.

This really needs thinking about and it is helpful, if not essential, to count the beats.

This manner of playing applies to all bourrées and minuets.

In these exercises you should match the turns to the note values.

Note value	Turns of the wheel
♩	½
𝅗𝅥	1
𝅗𝅥.	1½

Exercise 1
Give half a turn for each crotchet

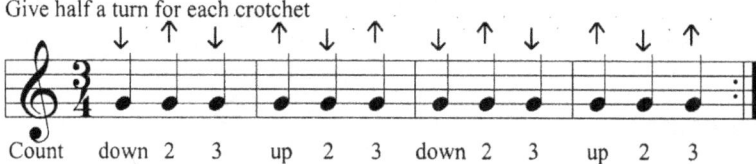

Count   down 2   3   up 2   3   down 2   3   up 2   3

Exercise 2
Use chanterelle(s) only, at first; then with the trompette, giving half a turn to each crotchet

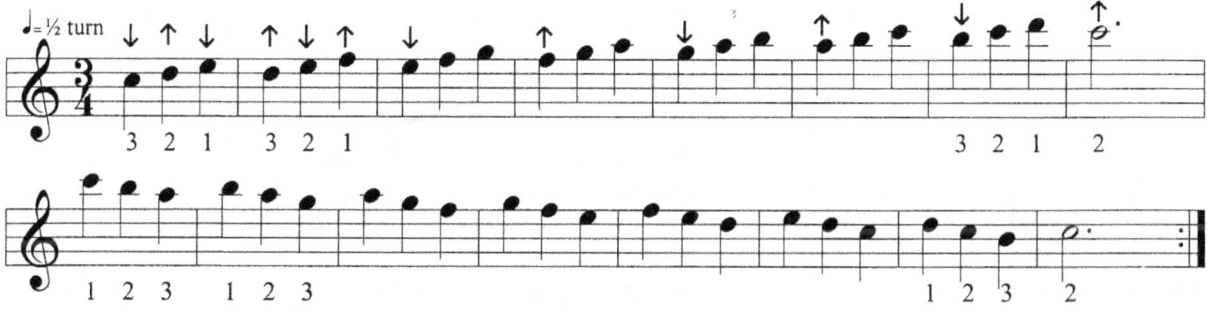

When the piece begins with the third beat, start with the knob at the bottom and at the end also finish with the knob at the bottom.

To play the first bar of Exercise 3 start with the knob at the top, give a sharp down-stroke, and glide round 1½ times, ending at the bottom. Sound the trompette only at the point 1 and not at points 2 and 3.

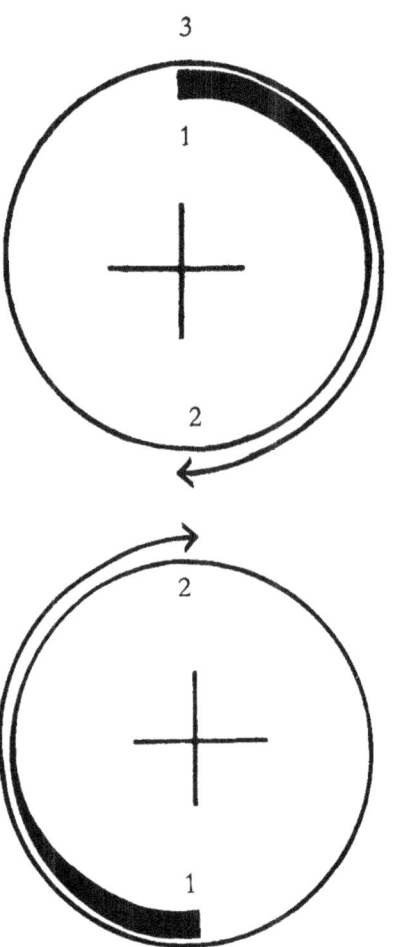

To play the second bar, start at the bottom, give an up-stroke and glide round 1½ times, finishing at the top. Continue thus, starting alternate bars at the top and at the bottom.

Exercise 3

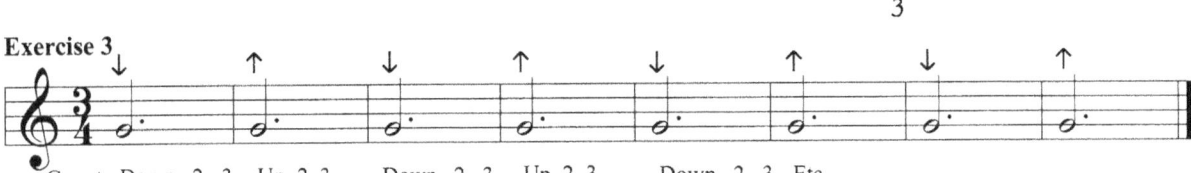

Count: Down 2 3   Up 2 3   Down 2 3   Up 2 3   Down 2 3   Etc

Exercise 4
Start with a down-stroke

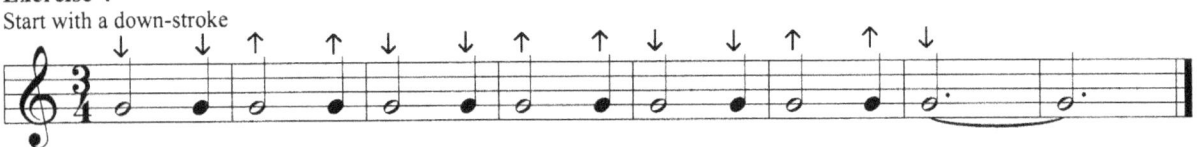

Exercise 5
N.B. The knob should be at the top when you finish

Exercise 6
A tune in 3/4 time

It was usual in the 18th century to start a bar of triple time with an up-stroke. This way is better because the last note of the phrase, which is a strong beat, then falls on the down-stroke.

JOLIVÉTÉ ET BONE AMOURS ♩ = ½ turn

13th century trouvère song

When a piece of music has the time signature 3/8 it is played with the same turns of the wheel as a quick piece with the time signature of 3/4, but in this case there are three quavers to the beat instead of three crotchets, and you give half a turn of the wheel for each quaver.

The turns depend upon the speed of the movement. For a gigue, bourrée or minuet do the turns as in the diagram opposite.

Note value	Turns of the wheel
♪	½
♩	1
♩.	1½

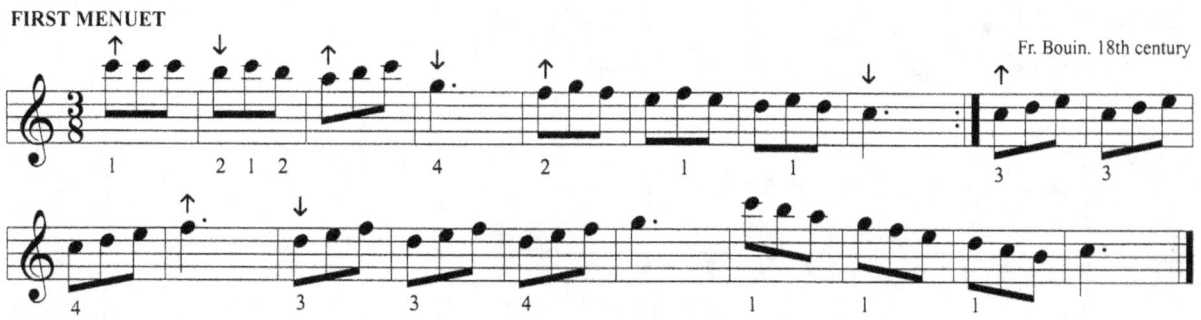

FIRST MENUET

Fr. Bouin. 18th century

LESSON 4
The irregular two-stroke
Le coup de deux irrégulier

There are two kinds of irregular two-stroke.

The first one begins with the down-stroke, using the thumb, for a quarter of a turn, which brings the knob level with the soundboard, followed by another down-stroke for the remaining three-quarters, gliding to the point of departure at the top.

Exercise 1

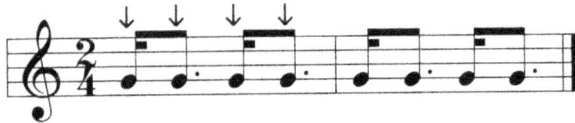

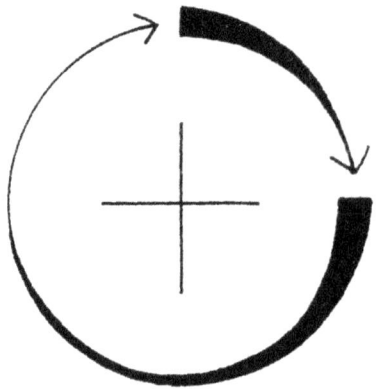

Two buzzes in one turn; a short one and a long one.

The second kind is more often used.

This begins with the down-stroke, gliding for three-quarters of a turn, until the knob is level with the soundboard, and finishes with an up-stroke for the last quarter of a turn.

Exercise 2a

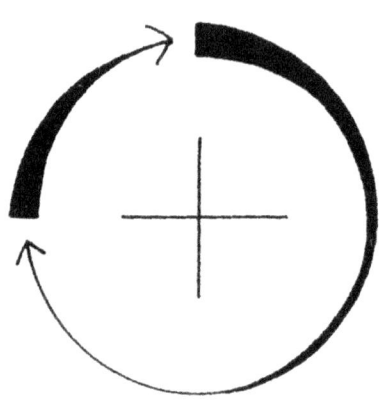

A long one and a short one.

Practise it also in this way:

Begin with a quarter-turn up-stroke, followed by the three-quarters down-stroke. This must be practised very neatly and carefully. It may be helpful to count the semi-quavers while doing it.

Exercise 2b

Exercise 3

> **TIP**
> This stroke is made easier if, at the 9 o'clock position, you twist the wrist slightly and briskly to the right. This causes the hand to twist, thus raising the end of the 2nd finger which makes the stroke.

Exercise 4
Synchronising the two hands

Exercise 5
In 2/2 each minim takes one turn, each bar has two turns.

Semibreve = 2 turns

LES MOUTONS

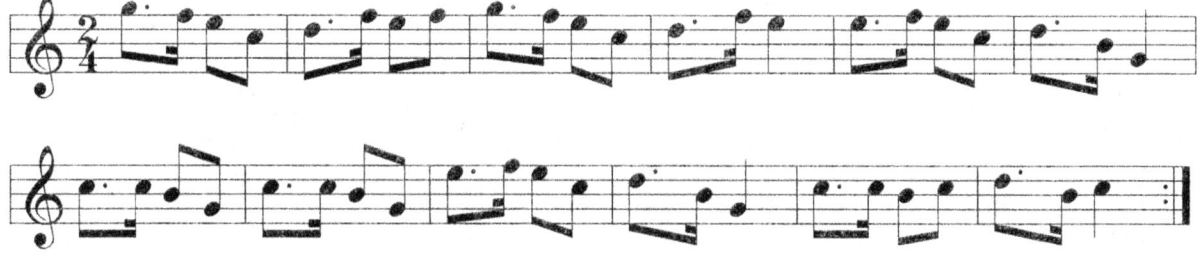

LA CHÈVRE

LA BOURRÉE DES DINDES

In this 18th century piece for hurdy-gurdy and cello
the trills must start on the upper note and on the beat.

LE MIRLITON

Second collection. Chédeville L'Aîné

LESSON 5A
The first irregular three-stroke
Le premier coup de trois irrégulier

Start at the top, with a small down-stroke for the first quarter turn. Give another down-stroke for the second quarter turn. The 3rd stroke is done with the third finger, and is the same as the up-stroke in the two-stroke.

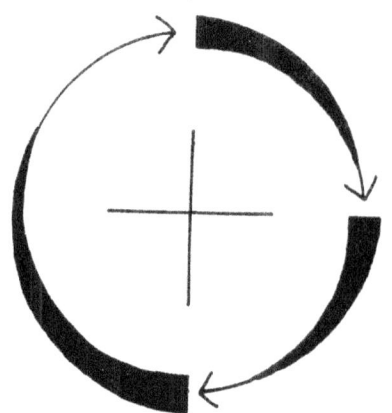

Exercise 1a   ♪ = ½ turn

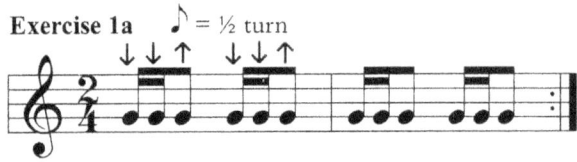

Exercise 1b   ♩ = ½ turn

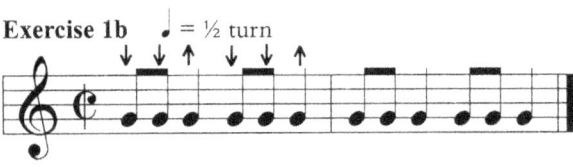

Exercise 2
Synchronising the two hands. Duple time.

3 2 1   3 2 1   3 2 1   1 2 3

Exercise 3
Triple time   ♩ = ½ turn

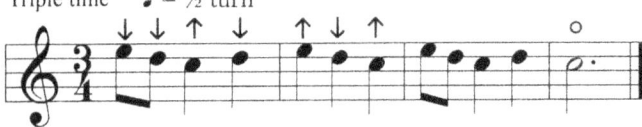

LA BOURRÉE VILLEBRET   ♪ = ½ turn

LA MONTAGNARDE

Tempo de Valse   Bourrée Auvergnate

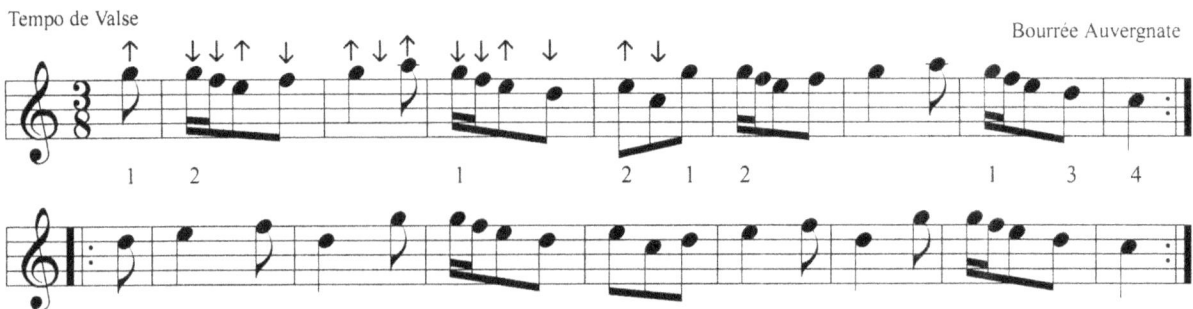

LESSON 5B
The second irregular three-stroke
Le second coup de trois irrégulier

Starting at the top, give a down-stroke for the first half turn, and two quarter-turn up-strokes.

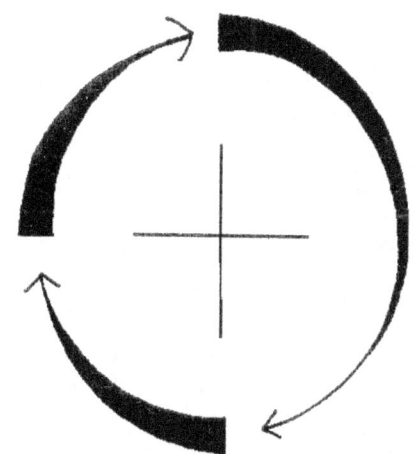

Exercise 4

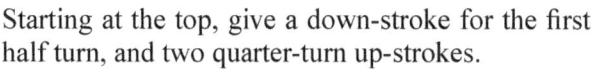

Exercise 5
Synchronising the two hands

RONDEAU Duet

Chédeville l'Aîné

Gaiment

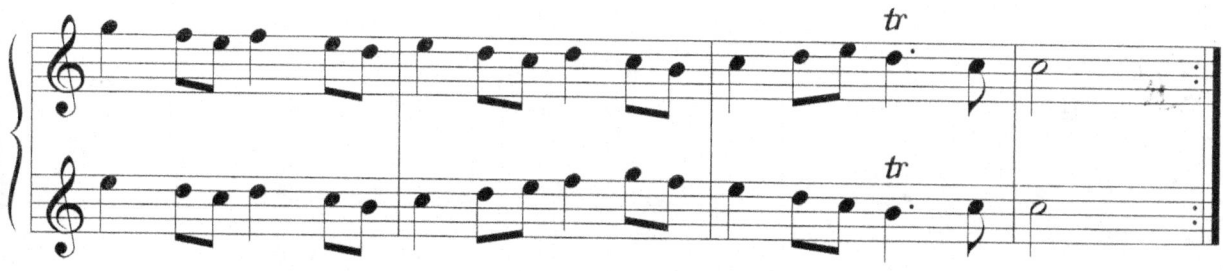

L'AGEASSE

47

LESSON 6
The regular four-stroke
Le coup de quatre régulier

Make two strokes descending and two strokes ascending. The four-stroke is made up of the movements of the two previous turns you have learnt. But it is not easy at first and you must practise slowly and meticulously so as to make the accents in exactly the right part of the wheel.

Listen carefully in order to check that the four accents are of equal strength.

To begin with, the speed should be as slow as one stroke per second, breaking up the rotation of the wheel into four separate movements. Gradually increase the tempo, aiming to have a relaxed hand and arm to keep the movement of the wheel continuous and gliding between the strokes.

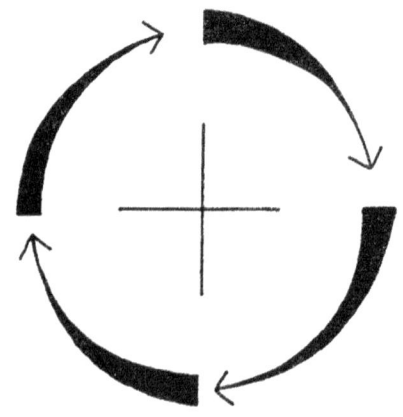

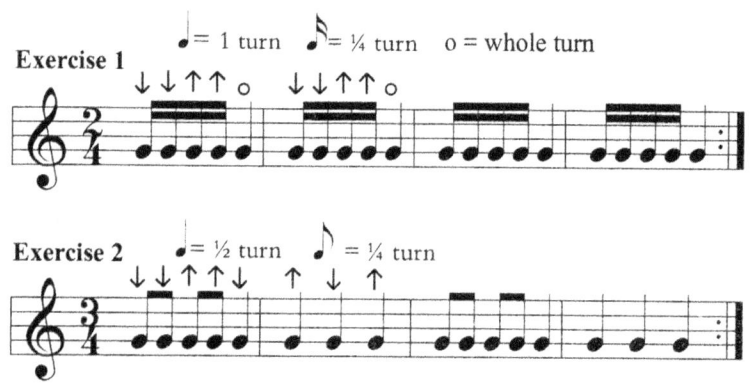

Do not *push* the handle around the circle, but aim short, light blows at it, from the four contact points on your hand, each point sending it in a different direction as described. Refer to page 31.

More exercises for the four-stroke Practice these starting with the upstroke as well as the downstroke.

LA BOURRÉE DE LASCROUX

LA POLKA PIQUÉE

LESSON 7
The regular three-stroke
Le coup de trois régulier

This stroke is used for pieces in 6/8, 9/8, 12/8, 6/4. You may find this easier than the four-stroke.

Start with the knob at the top. Rotate the wheel through one third of a turn, striking down with the thumb.

The second stroke is made by striking the knob towards you with the tip of the second finger. The third stroke is an up-stroke using the end joint of the third finger.

Use as a guide to positioning the wheel, the two buttons to which the leather straps are attached, and the handle at the top, making a triangle.

Make the three strokes very precise and equal.

These strokes correspond to three quavers in 6/8, 9/8 or 12/8 time, or three crotchets in 6/4.

The ♩. = 1 whole turn, or one beat.

The 18th century players called this the *coup perdu*.

Practise the following rhythm, taking care not to let 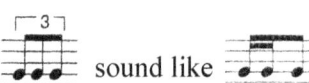 sound like

Exercise 1

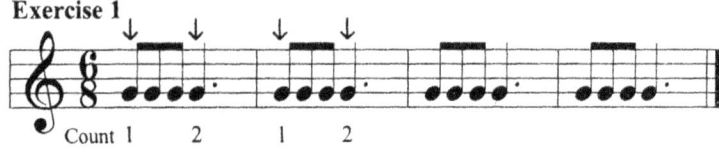

Also count 1 2 3 4 5 6, 1 2 3 4 5 6

Saying the words of this old nursery rhyme should help establish the rhythm.

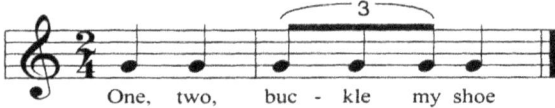

The group of three quavers with a 3 over it is called a triplet when in 2/4, 3/4 or 4/4 time, and must be played in the time of one crotchet.

Exercise 2

AUPRES DE MA BLONDE

D.C. = Da Capo. Go back to the beginning

LILLIBURLERO

The "limping" stroke
Le coup de boiteux

In 6/8 time (compound duple time) we use the following turns of the wheel:

Rhythm	Note value	Turns of the wheel	
♩ ♪ ♩ ♪		Either	or*
	♩.	1 turn	1 turn
	♩	½ turn	2/3 turn
	♪	½ turn also, but more rapidly	1/3 turn

* Some players prefer to divide the wheel-turn in the second way.

Exercise 3

When the quaver is one of three ♪♪♪ and there are no semi-quavers, its value is one third of a turn and we use the regular 3-stroke. This is faster than the 3/8 piece in Lesson 3 (Menuet, page 43). If there are semi-quavers you must use half turns and quarter turns. This applies to most bourrées.

Exercise 4

THE MILLER OF DEE — Traditional English

THE KEEL ROW

FANFARE — New collection. Chedeville l'Aîné

This piece sounds equally good in C minor.

When the rhythm is dotted and the music is quick and gay, we use the following turns of the wheel:

Exercise 5

Rhythm	Note value	Turns of the wheel	
♩. ♫		A	B
	♩.	1 turn	1
	♩	½ turn	½
	♪.	¼ turn, played long	3/8
	♬	¼ turn, played more rapidly	1/8
	♪	½ turn	½

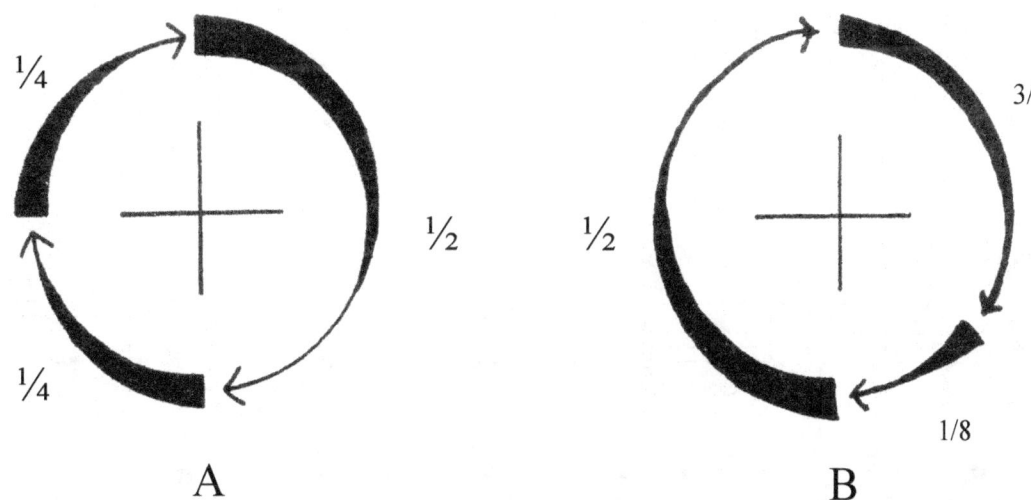

A   B

Some players prefer to divide the wheel the second way.

---

trill ∿ see page 71
D.S. = Go back to the sign
al Fine = To the end (Fine)

JENNY PLUCK PEARS

Playford
Dorian mode

This piece begins with with the equal 3-stroke, then changes to 3/4, for which you use the 2-stroke.

Marmotte

Songs like this, with their mixture of German and French words, were probably sung by itinerant vielle players of Savoy, who often carried pet marmottes with them, little furry, brown animals (not monkeys) found in northern Europe, as seen in the picture opposite, held by the little boy.

The words were adapted by Goethe, and Beethoven set it as a song with piano accompaniment.

It is more effective not to use the regular three-stroke, but to mark only the first of the two slurred quavers with the *trompette*, and mark both the semi-quavers.

MARMOTTE

Beethoven

Ich kom - me schon durch man - ches Land, a - vec - que la mar - mot - te, und im - mer was zu es - sen fand, a - vec - que la mar - mot - te, a - vec - que si, a - vec - que la, a - vec - que la mar - mot - te, a - vec - que si, a - vec - que la, a - vec - que la mar - mot - te.

Departure of the little Savoyards (19th century)

LESSON 8
The irregular four-stroke
le coup de quatre irrégulier

This is used for the dotted or skipping rhythm in tunes which are very light and quick in character, and where the irregular two stroke would give too strong and heavy a sound. It is used for the dance known as a 'Scottish' and also for the mazurka.

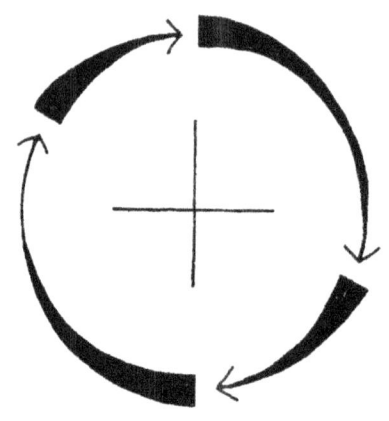

Rhythm	Note value	Turns of the wheel
♫. ♫.	♩	½
	♫.	½
	♪.	3/8
	♪	1/8

Exercise 1

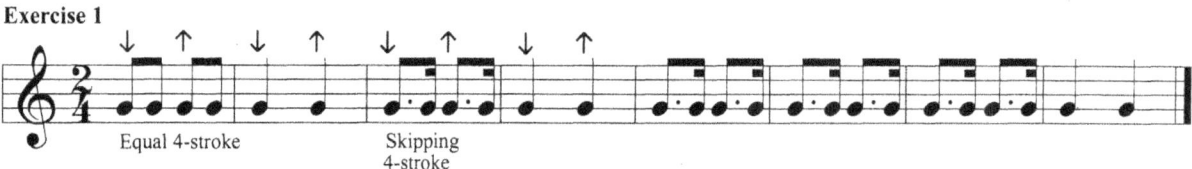

Equal 4-stroke   Skipping 4-stroke

SCOTTISH-VALSE

LA VIEILLE SCOTTISH

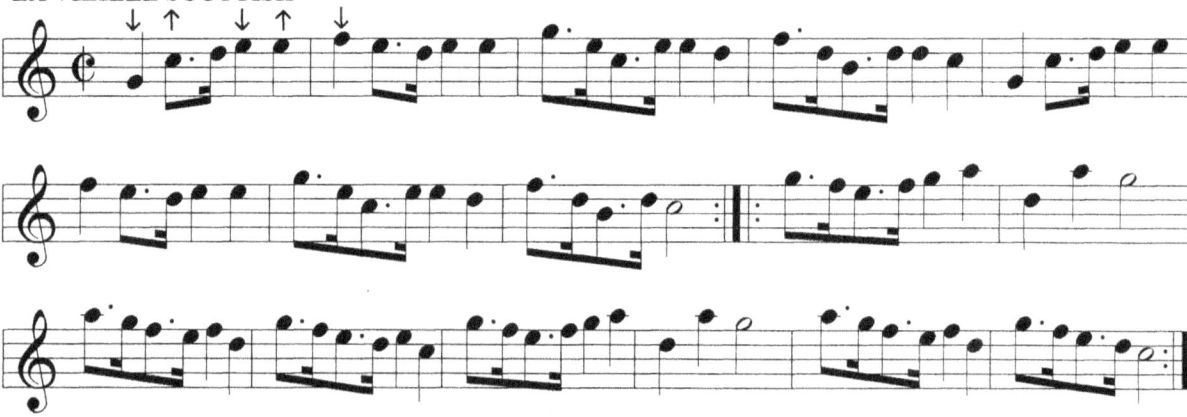

Vieille means 'old' and is pronounced vee-ay`-ee.

St. Chartier hurdy-gurdy dance group

LESSON 9
The six-stroke and the eight-stroke
Le coup de six et le coup de huit

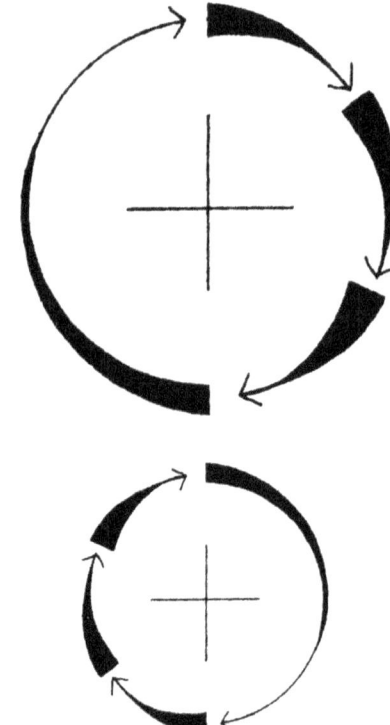

With time, patience, skill and a well-adjusted trompette, there is no reason why any hurdy-gurdy player should not be able to master six or even eight strokes or buzzes in one turn of the wheel as an extra embellishment over and above the demands of the music. It sounds fantastic.

You may, however, wish to do three strokes in half a turn for a triplet, either upwards or downwards.

The triplet
In simple time (2/4, 3/4) the crotchet beat is normally divided into two quavers, but when one finds an occasional crotchet sub-divided into three quavers with the number 3 over it, this group of notes is called a triplet and is played in the time of one crotchet.

The triplet should not be confused with the groups of three quavers in compound time, (6/8, 9/8, 12/8) which are equal to a dotted crotchet.

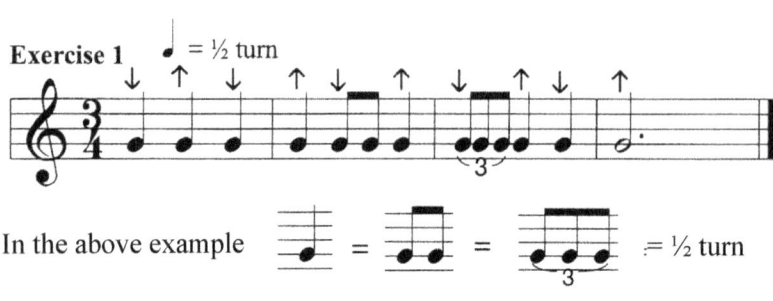

Rhythm	Note value	Turns of the wheel
♩ ♫♫₃	♪	1/6
	♫♫₃	½ or 3/6
	♩	½

The manivelle must be held very lightly in order to give three strokes in half a turn, or the triplet may be slurred, giving one stroke on the first note of the triplet only.

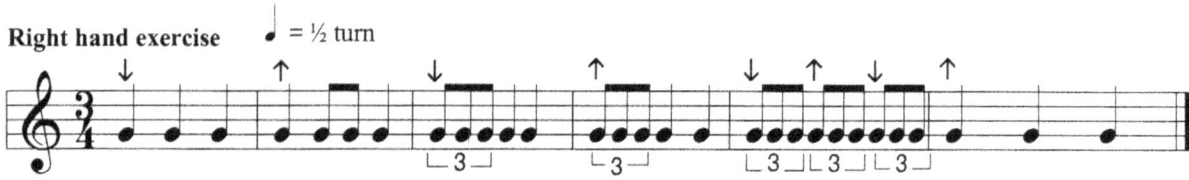

60

If the crotchet is given a whole turn, then one uses the regular three-stroke for the triplet, as in La Gigue and La Marche de Brive (see pages 89 and 90). But if the crotchet is given half a turn then the triplet has to be played in half a turn, ie, using half of the six-stroke.

SECOND MENUET

Bouin Method

MARCH FROM THE PEASANTS' WEDDING

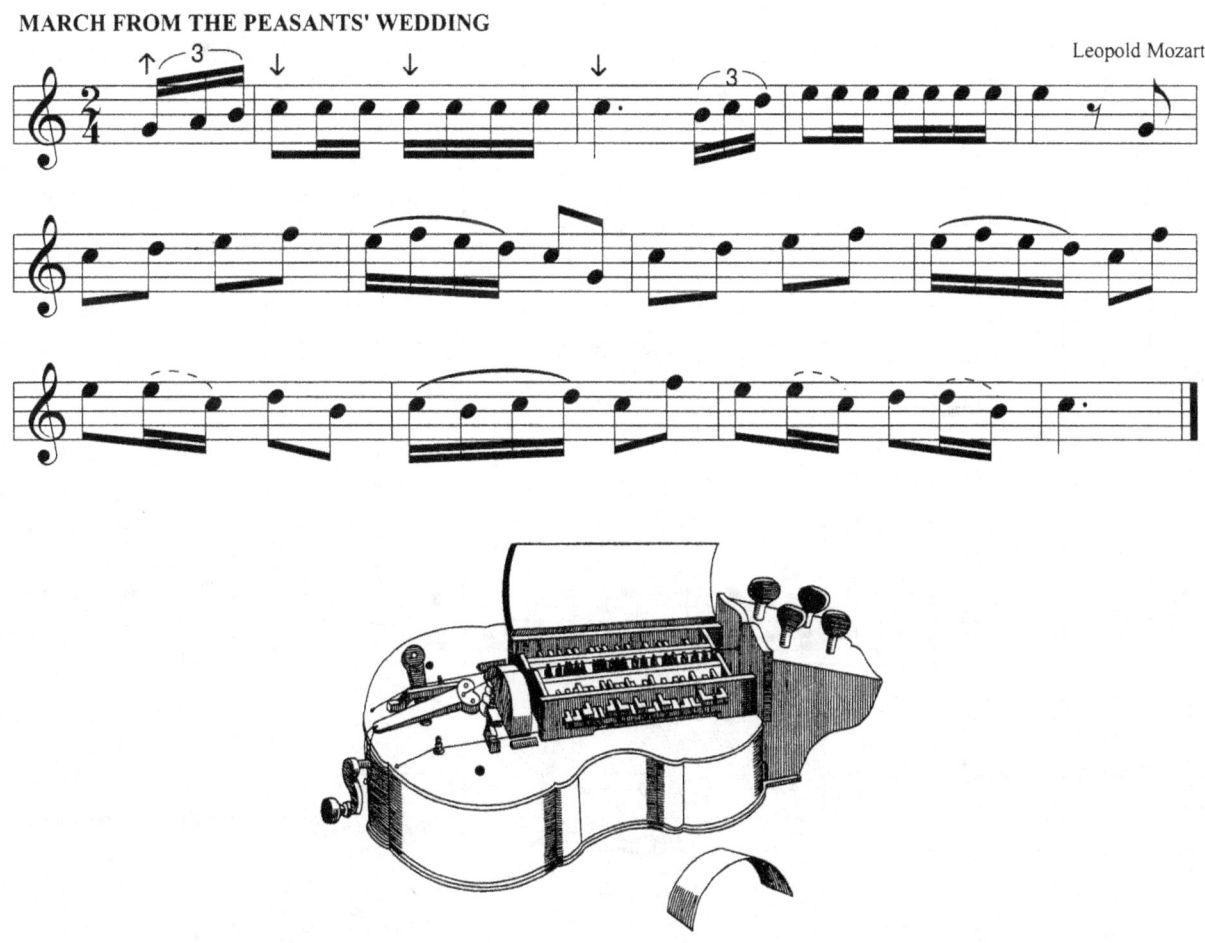

Leopold Mozart

A Hungarian hurdy-gurdy

PLAYING IN THE KEY OF G

When a piece has a key signature of one sharp and has G as its final note, it is in G major; G minor has two flats. If there are no sharps or flats, e.g. Cantiga de Santa Maria, page 84, but it ends on G, it is in the Mixolydian mode, the natural mode of the hurdy-gurdy, as it is of the Scottish bagpipe. (See pages 82-3.)

Use the *gros bourdon* (G), *mouche* (g), tune the trompette up a tone to D and readjust the trompette.

It is convenient to have a small key fitted to the soundboard so that the trompette peg in the tail-piece does not need to be adjusted.

See also page 11.

PLAYING IN G MINOR

This has a key signature of two flats, and should not be confused with C minor, which has three flats, but is sometimes written with two. Check the key-note at the end of the piece. See Prelude in G minor, page 70. For the scale fingerings see page 27.

OÙ SONT DONC CES AMANTS?

CHER SILVANDRE 8th Collection. Chédeville L'Aîné

In the early 18th century the final flat of the key signature was usually omitted and placed in the text where necessary. See pages 71-72 for the meaning of +. Various ornaments may be used.

PLAYING IN C MINOR

One can change without a break from playing in C major to C minor because the drones remain the same. But the key signature has three flats: B, E and A. Sometimes the B flat is raised to B natural (the leading note), and only two flats are given in the key signature. Very often in the 18th century suites a dance tune in C major is followed by another in C minor, after which the first one is repeated. It is sometimes effective to heighten the contrast between the two pieces by playing the minor one with less frequent use of the trompette, giving it a more legato character.

7. Running 3rds.

Prelude

Other pieces in C minor
See also on page 54 The Miller of Dee, and on page 56 Jenny Pluck Pears and Marmotte
Aunt Rhodie on page 38 may also be played in C minor.

LA JEUNE ISABELLE
2nd Collection. Chédeville L'Ainé

NOEL: JOSEPH EST BIEN MARIÉ
French carol

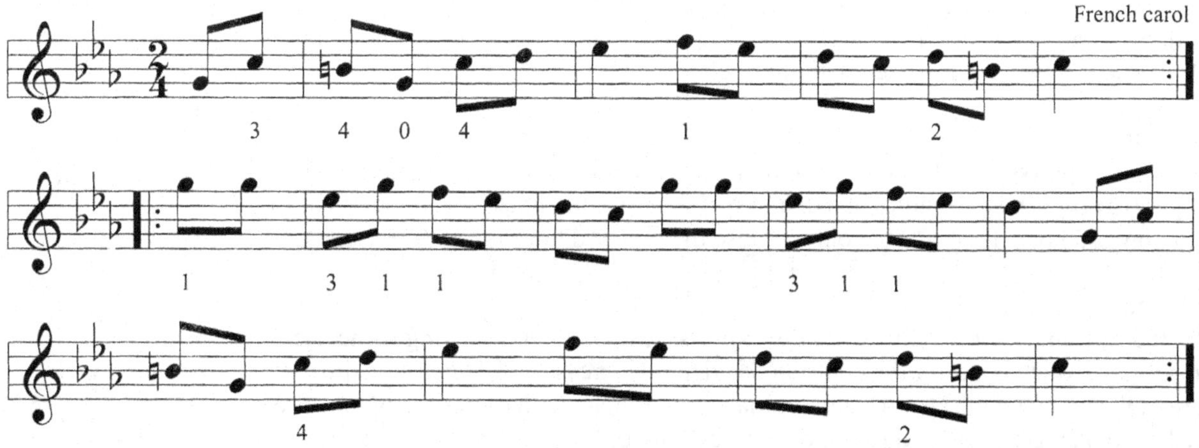

DIE ROMMELPOT
Flemish

STYLE AND INTERPRETATION

Tied notes
If two notes of the same degree are tied, you buzz only the first note with the trompette and glide for the value of the second note, keeping the finger down.

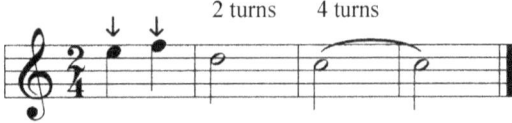

Slurs
If two or more notes of different degree are joined with a slur, articulate only the first note of the group, and complete the remaining turns of the wheel by gliding.
 The articulations may be given with the fingers or the wheel, or both, depending on circumstances and taste. If quavers are slurred in pairs the first may be played slightly longer than the second (*notes inégales*).

The pause ⌒
Give one or more extra turns of the wheel to lengthen the note, gradually slowing it down if it is the final note so as to get softer. The final note should taper off slightly or finish as usual with the knob at the top. Do not finish with an extra loud buzz, as this is unmusical.

Accents > v
Accentuate the note by making the buzz, or stroke, shorter and brisker, or by doubling the turns of the wheel.

Nuances
It is possible to observe the signs *p* (soft), *f* (loud), crescendo and diminuendo by increasing or decreasing the speed of the wheel. ⟨⟩
Both the * and the U are used by Baptiste Dupuit to indicate crescendo and diminuendo. The trompette is not used with these effects.

Triplets
Three notes played in the time of two. It is very difficult, if not impossible, for some players to articulate three notes in half a turn of the wheel in quick 2/4 time. In this case you may articulate the first note only, or else the first and third notes. (see Lesson 9)

Vibrato
Another technique which can add to the expressiveness of one's playing is the use of the vibrato, which is a carefully controlled and rapid increase and decrease of the pressure of the finger on the key. The finger maintains contact with the string by means of the key and tangent, and makes use of the elasticity of the string to give minute variations of pitch. But if the pressure should be too great the note will sound out of tune

Turning the wheel freely
There are some pieces, usually slow or expressive, which sound best entirely without the trompette.In other pieces you may want to play certain sections, or even a whole piece, first without the trompette and then with it, as a contrast. In this case disengage the trompette string and turn the wheel in a free style, going faster or slower to make the crescendos and diminuendos (louder and softer).
   When you are working on the fingering of a new piece, or learning the notes, let the

Syncopation
When the accent is shifted forward from a strong to a weak beat, that is known as syncopation. In the following example the accents are made by down-strokes falling on the notes indicated with an arrow, while the tied notes are held on with an unaccented turn of the wheel, giving a feel of two beats in the bar, instead of three.
See also Menuet, page 61.

Rests
When playing alone or when playing folk music it is normal to keep turning the wheel for the duration of the rest, so as not to jar the ear by the sudden ceasing of the drones.

However, in certain pieces, such as sonatas or concertos with other instruments, it may be necessary to stop on account of the harmony or the phrasing. You may find that after a particular rest the wheel is in the wrong position for starting the next note. In this case you must cut short the turn given to the note preceding the rest.

Playing on a single chanterelle
There is a style of playing the hurdy-gurdy using the principal chanterelle only, without trompette or drone strings, which can be strikingly effective when contrasted with the normal method of playing. One separates the notes by stopping the wheel, and by finger articulation. A skilful player can perform six, eight, or more semi-quavers per turn of the wheel, using this technique.

It is necessary to have a fine instrument with a sweet tone, and the aim is to make it sound like a violin. It is possible to play expressively by means of dynamic nuances, which are achieved by acceleration and deceleration of the wheel, and with rallentandos and rubatos.

Rests can be observed and phrases may be shaped, using slurs, staccato notes and accents. In addition one may use a vibrato by varying the pressure of the fingers of the left hand - which are in indirect contact with the string via the key and tangent. This vibrato should be used with restraint and taste, and should not be constant.

HOW TO PLAY EIGHTEENTH CENTURY MUSIC ON THE VIELLE

At first sight the hurdy-gurdy would appear to be rather an unsuitable instrument for the performance of baroque music, whose characteristics are essentially elegance, grace, and subtlety of expression.

Nevertheless, French composers in the eighteenth century wrote a great deal of charming and enjoyable music for the vielle which overcame its apparent limitations.

The hurdy-gurdy as a folk instrument, with its insistent and penetrating trompette is loud, forceful and brilliant, giving a strong rhythm which is essential for the dance.

A completely different approach is needed for the courtly dances of the eighteenth century, particularly for the slow airs, minuets and musettes. A whole book would be necessary to explain baroque style in detail, but there is room here for a brief summary of the essential principles.

No.1 Use a small eighteenth or early nineteenth century French instrument or a copy of one, or string your hurdy-gurdy more lightly and use a quieter trompette. The guitar-shaped instruments are better than the lute-shaped ones as the tone is clearer and more delicate. You should use an instrument tuned to G/C.

No. 2 Learn to use the trompette with discretion and not all the time, nor on every note.

No. 3 Understand the character and mood of each piece and its correct tempo, and use the trompette accordingly. For example, use it less in slow and expressive pieces and more in quick pieces which have a strong rhythm.

No. 4 Learn to articulate the phrases so as to make the shape and form of the music clear, by stopping the wheel when necessary, and also by using suitable fingering, so as to have breathing spaces as in a song.

No. 5 Feel the rise and fall of tension in each musical phrase, and increase or diminish the speed of the wheel so as to play more loudly or softly, and double the turns of the wheel to stress certain long notes.

No. 6 Bring out the form of a piece by playing different sections in a contrasting style, i.e. by using more or less staccato, for example, in a minor key minuet following a major one, or in the repeated sections of a rondo.

No. 7 Learn to use the essential grace notes naturally and easily (i.e. those normally printed printed above the notes or in small type) and to use additional ornaments where your fancy takes you, and to give variety and personal expression to your performance.

An aristocratic lady playing her vielle. 18th century painting.

No. 8 Know when to play pairs of quavers or semi-quavers unequal (*louré*) although they are written equal. In music of slow and medium tempo groups of consecutive notes of the smallest value are normally played unequal, two by two, the first longer and the second shorter. Usually composers did not indicate where notes should be played unequal as it was left to the good taste of the player, but when notes are slurred in pairs this usually indicates inequality. See *Les Bergeries*, by Couperin, page 74.

The degree of inequality cannot easily be notated, as it consists of prolonging or leaning on the first note, sometimes as if it were dotted and sometimes less. As François Couperin said:

> "We write a thing differently from the way in which we execute it; and it is this which causes foreigners to play our music less well than we do theirs. For instance, we dot several consecutive quavers in diatonic succession, and yet we write them as equal."

The 18th century Methods

The Methods by Baptiste Dupuit (1741) and François Bouin (1761) are the most helpful and informative if one wishes to make a detailed study of the style and techniques of playing in the eighteenth century. They both give numerous musical examples and exercises to illustrate the text, and Dupuit includes a section on musical taste or style (*le goût*) as well as a set of sonatas with notes on the performance of each movement.

The Corette method is very short and contains little information, but it is valuable for the collection of charming pieces, including some for two vielles, some with figured bass* and some songs with vielle accompaniment.

* i.e. For the gamba and the harpsichord. These pieces are not included in the later 19th century edition in the British Library.

Title page of a set of suites for two musettes or vielles by Chédeville le Jeune.

MORE ABOUT FINGERING
The use of the thumb

Baptiste Dupuit in his *Principes pour toucher de la vielle* (1741) is the only teacher to suggest using the thumb in passages such as a sequence of five-note runs (Fig. 1) and in arpeggio or broken chord passages as in Fig. 2. The letter 'p' indicates the thumb (*pouce*). For alternatives to Fig. 1, not using the

Preluding

It was the custom in the 18th century to "warm up" with a prelude before playing a sonata in a concert. This prelude, which would be in the same key as the piece to follow, served to accustom the ear and the fingers to that key, and as it was designed to encompass all the notes on the instrument, in that key, it served to check that everything was working well and that all strings and tangents were well tuned and adjusted.

FOUR PRELUDES BY BOUIN
from *La Vielleuse Habile*

ORNAMENTATION IN EIGHTEENTH CENTURY MUSIC

The ornaments which the composer has placed over the notes are the essential ones. Additional ornaments may be used according to the player's fancy.

Fingering ornaments on the hurdy-gurdy
Try to start an ornament with the first finger or the second, rather than with any other, if necessary making a hand shift in order to do so. Move only the first finger to perform the repeated strokes of a trill, keeping the second finger on the key.

GRACE NOTES, OR ESSENTIAL ORNAMENTS

The trill (*cadence, tremblement, battement*)
Composers use various signs and names for this ornament. The most frequent signs are ⁀, t, tr, +. The last may mean any ornament of your choice.
The termination (the note which follows the dot) should always be extremely short, regardless of the written value, which is here a quaver but is played as a semi-quaver or less.

The detached trill
This stroke consists of only two finger repetitions on a note which moves down by step. It must always begin on the upper note, e,d,e,d and not d,e,d,e.

The tied trill
In this trill you must take care not to articulate the first grace note, which is tied. Hold the finger on the note preceding the trill so as to join them.

The turn
The grace notes are played more or less quickly just before the third beat.

The use of the trompette
Mark only the first note of an ornament with the trompette, in some cases shortening the note immediately before the ornament so as to leave a little rest or aspiration before the first note.

Rules for playing the trill
Play the preparation note on the beat with a downstroke. Glide the wheel during the finger-strokes until the rest, then mark the termination, which is always very short with a left hand finger staccato and an upstroke. The final note is played with a downstroke. If the value of the note allows, the speed of the trill must increase.

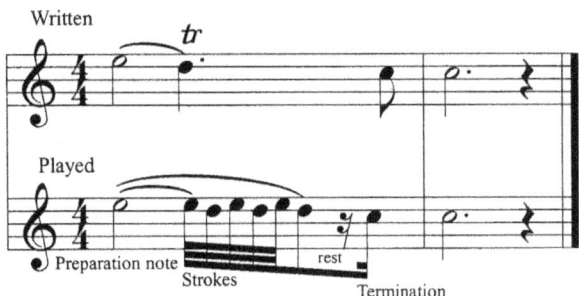

The trill followed by a turn

The final trill
This always begins by playing the note above the note to be ornamented, even though it is not actually written, and moreover, this invisible note takes half the value of the principal note.

**The mordent, lower mordent,
or *pincé simple***
A single alternation performed with the note below, or the note above, when it is called *martellement*. Begin on the principal note and strike the note below once very rapidly.
With two alternations it is called a double mordent. For the double mordent strike the lower note twice.

The inverted mordent or *martellement*
This is a short trill without preparation, beginning on the written note. One strikes the upper note once.

The appoggiatura or *Port de voix*
This is sometimes shown by a little added note and sometimes by the sign v.
The appoggiatura takes half the value of the note that follows it.

An appoggiatura can be joined to a mordent if it is on a fairly long note.
The appoggiatura is frequently followed by a mordent.

The passing appoggiatura or
Le port de voix passager
There are two kinds of passing appoggiatura. One kind (accented) should be sounded on the beat. The others, passing appoggiaturas (before the beat and unaccented) are found when a number of notes of the same value descend by leaps of a third. The grace notes are not accented.

Accented appoggiatura or *port de voix frappant*
These are found in front of a long downbeat that follows a short upbeat. The appoggiatura must be sustained for half of the following pricipal note. Appoggiaturas may approach from below or from above.

When the apoggiatura is applied to a dotted note it lasts two thirds of the value of the dotted note, while the principal note itself lasts only one third.

The *coulée*
When one finds a sequence of descending thirds, these may be filled by playing intermediate notes, slurring them two by two, taking care to lift the finger off the second note. Do not accent the grace notes.

The *coulade*
The coulade is indicated by several little notes, consecutive, ascending or descending, which are played without interrupting the rhythm or melodic line and without accenting.

The crescendo
A crescendo can be made by gradually turning the wheel more and more quickly. Obviously, the crescendo and diminuendo cannot be used with the trompette.

This piece is from *La Vielleuse Habile* by Fr. Bouin and gives his fingerings and instructions.

In Couperin's original harpsichord piece the last three notes of bar two are written as a triplet and the preceding note is a crotchet.

Rondo form: A, B, A, C, A, D, A, E, A

MUSETTE Bertin

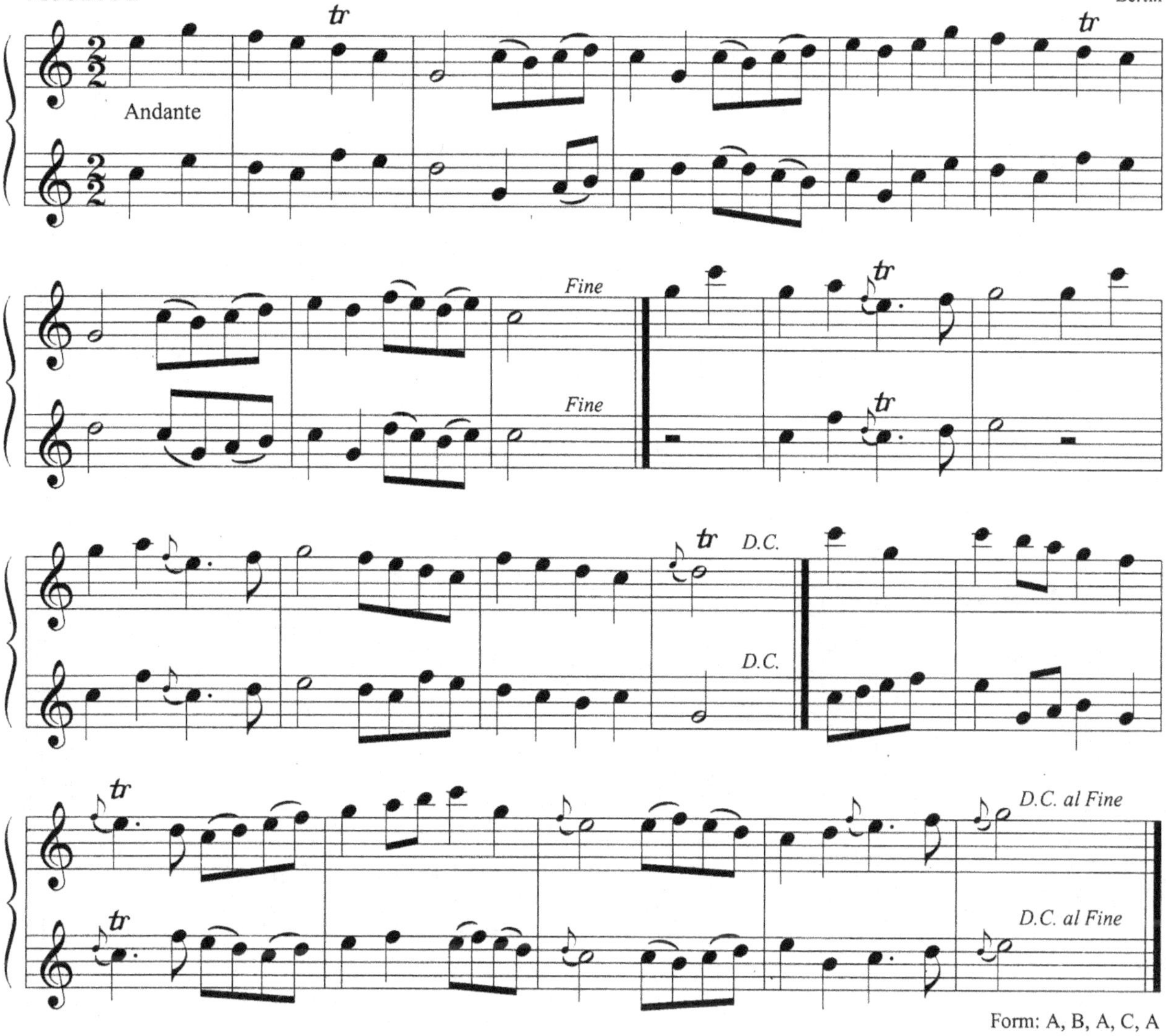

Andante
tr
Fine
D.C.
D.C. al Fine

Form: A, B, A, C, A

The following remark is made by Bouin: "On quavers one must press the finger more strongly for the long quavers and less strongly for the short ones." This is a reference to '*notes inégales*' (see page 66) and applies in this piece to the slurred quavers.

Musettes should be played smoothly and without trompette.

EXERCISES FOR THE TRILL

Hold down 2 and repeat 1
tr
Effect

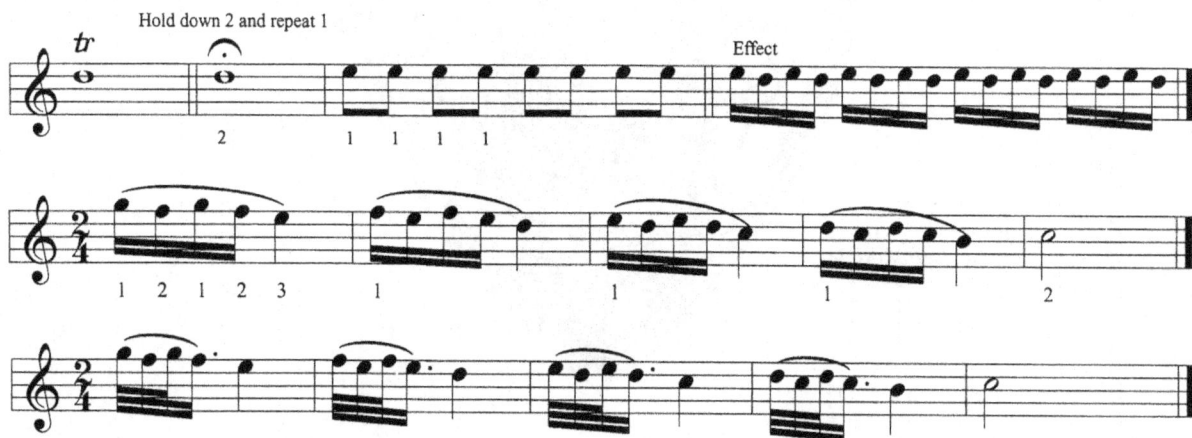

This brisk dance needs the trompette on every note.

RIGAUDON J.B. Boismortier

Design from a gingerbread mould
Bagpiper and hurdy-gurdy player
Slovakia (18th. century)

Exercises by Fr. Bouin (1761)

Exercises by Hubert Marcheix

1. Thirds

2. Fourths

THE MEDIAEVAL SYMPHONY AND ORGANISTRUM

Detail of box-symphony showing keys with two positions for some tangents

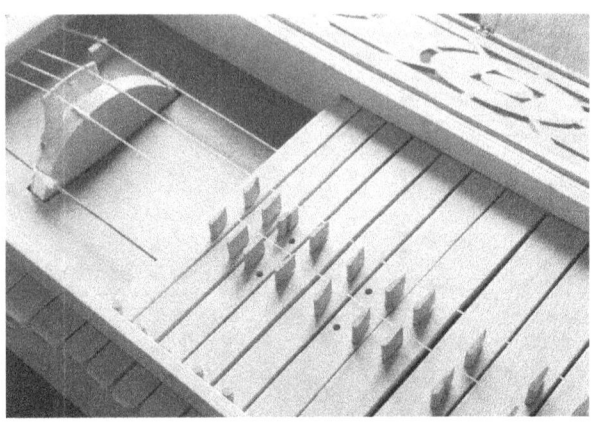

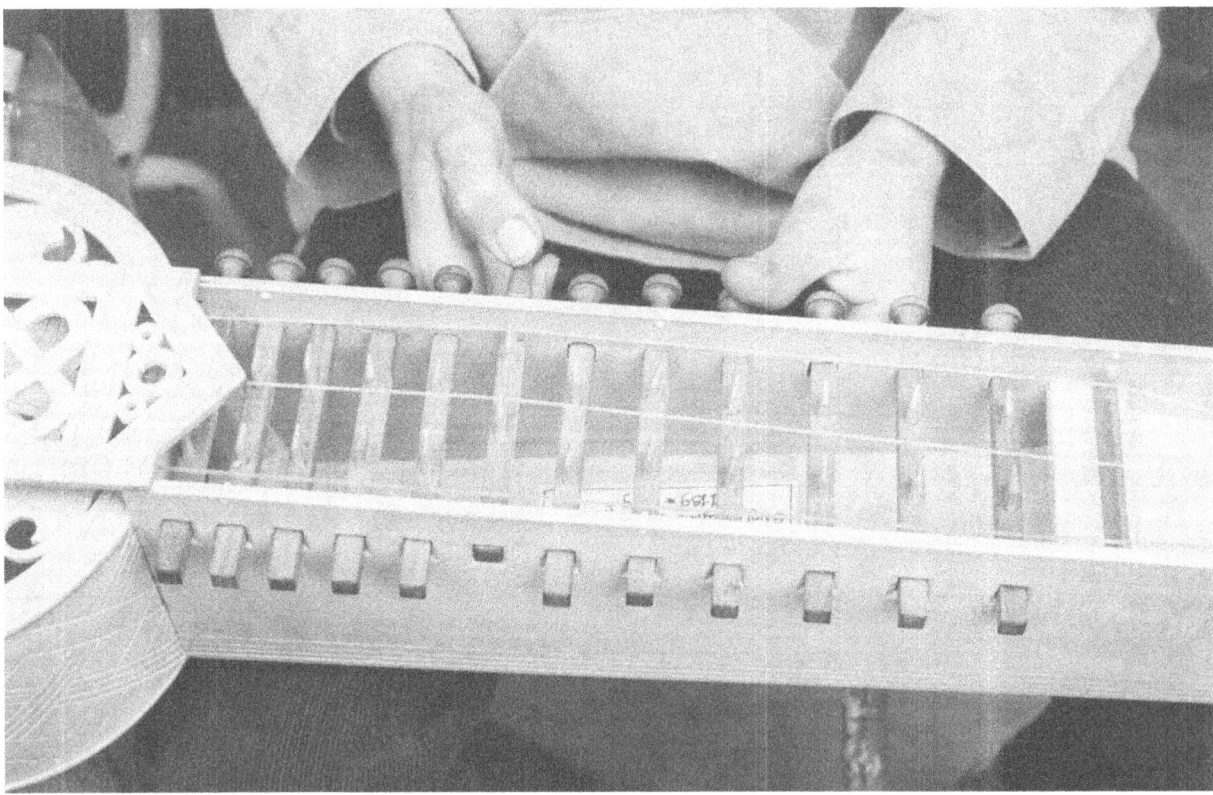

Playing a realisation of the organistrum of Santiago de Compostela, with the keybox cover slid back to show the tangents. (Also see page 3.)

THE MEDIAEVAL SYMPHONY

The name 'symphony' has come to be used nowadays to describe mediæval hurdy-gurdies of the rectangular box type, as shown in the picture reproduced on this page, but one should remember that the name 'symphony' was used until the eighteenth century in France, and referred to many different forms of the instrument.

The mediæval symphonies, which were basically monochords, were almost certainly diatonic, having few or no sharps or flats, and were usually shown to have only three strings, as evidenced by the tuning pegs.

We do not really know how the symphony was strung or tuned. No doubt there were various methods and today, as in the past, the musician will vary it according to the needs of the music. It is unlikely that the *trompette*, or vibrating bridge, was incorporated in the symphony in the thirteenth century, and it is generally thought to have been a later addition (as a similar trembling bridge appeared on the monochord or tromba marina at the end of the fifteenth century). Some makers today, however, fit it to their 'mediæval' symphonies, together with a chromatic keyboard, but this alters its charming simplicity. The symphony is a very easy instrument to play, and presents few problems to the beginner.

Strings and tuning
The symphony illustrated at the top of page 78 has proved to be very useful for the performance of mediaeval music, and is strung as follows:
  2 melody strings (violin A) tuned to G.
  1st drone string (bass viol 5th) tuned to C.
  2nd drone string (bass viol 6th) tuned to G.

The B and F keys have two sets of holes for the tangents, giving one the choice of B flat or B natural and F natural or F sharp. This avoids the necessity for having another row of keys for accidentals, and so makes fingering easier. Most mediæval tunes are modal and have a small compass, so that by re-tuning one or other of the drone strings, melodies in every mode fit easily on the keyboard, which has a range of one and a half octaves.

For the techniques of playing, tuning and regulating the symphony, which are the same as for the modern hurdy-gurdy, see pages 10-13.

Miniature from the Cantigas de Santa Maria (13th century)

CHANSON DE MAI (C drone) — Monniot d'Arras

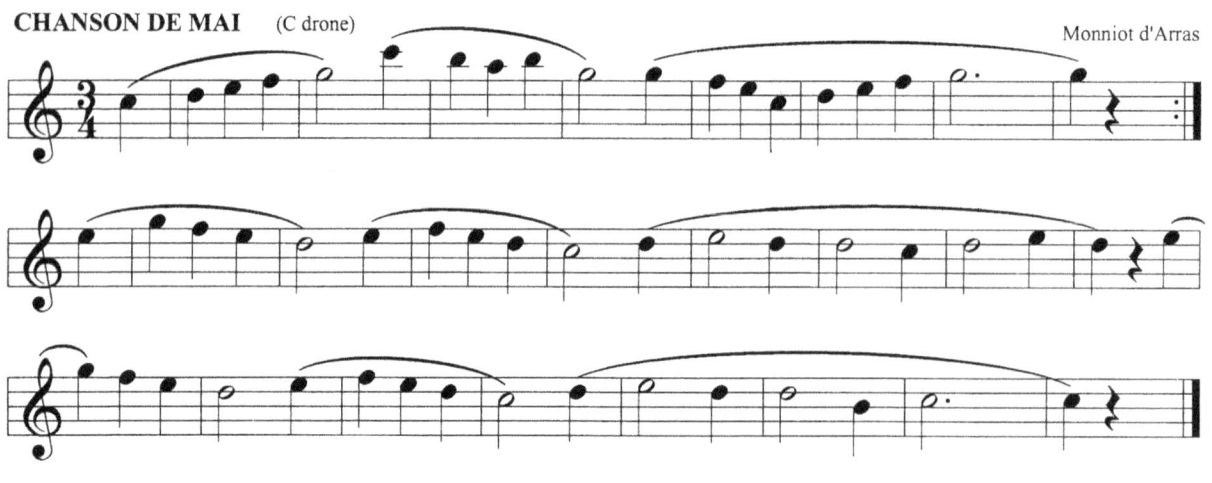

DUCTIA (G drone)   Lively dance — 14th century

QUAND JE VOY IVER RETORNER (C drone) Slow — Colin Muset

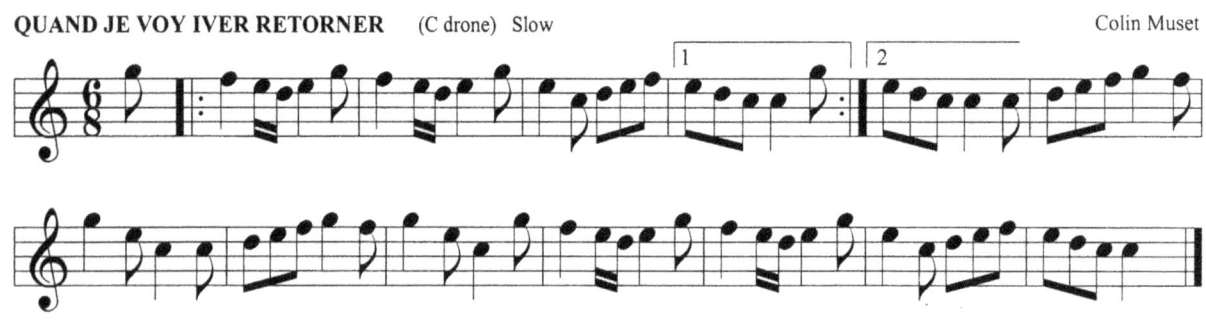

LAMENTO DI TRISTANO (E drone. No trompette)   Slow dance

A mediæval minstrel arrives to entertain a noble lord at his table.
French miniature of the Romance of Girart de Nevers.

MODES

a) The six modes, one on each of the natural keys, except B.

b) All starting on C, using sharps or flats to correct the positions of the semi-tones.

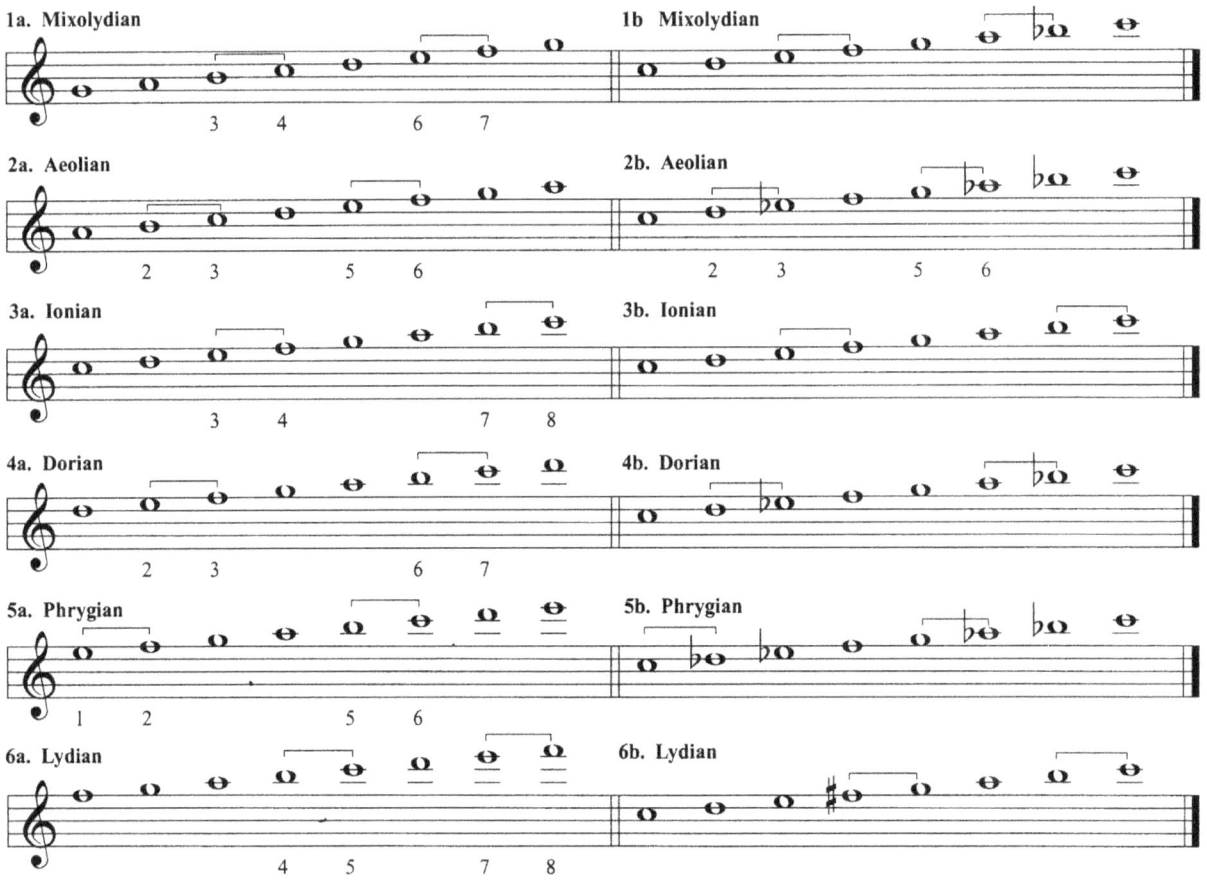

Four extra positions for a hurdy-gurdy or other instrument with only a B flat and F sharp.

SCALES AND MODES

When playing a drone instrument such as the hurdy-gurdy, the bagpipes or the appalachian dulcimer, it is essential to know which note of the melody to choose as the drone. It is nearly always the final note. This can be doubled an octave or two octaves lower. Usually the 5th note above this bottom drone can be used in addition, but this doesn't work for all tunes.

If one plays a series of eight notes ascending using only the naturals (black keys on the hurdy-gurdy), and starting each time on a different note, one will discover the mediæval modes, which are still to be found in folk music today and particularly in bagpipe tunes. Each mode has a different character, because of the different positions of the tones and semi-tones in relation to the final. The semitones are indicated by a bracket. (See examples 1-6)

The same modes are shown transposed, all with C as the final, this time using sharps or flats to correct the intervals.

The Ionian mode is our modern major scale. The most commonly used modes in mediæval and folk music are the Dorian, Aeolian and Mixolydian. However, there are many examples of the Phrygian mode in Spain and the Lydian mode in Slovakia.

On a chromatic instrument any of these modes may be played using G or C as the final.

On a diatonic instrument, a copy of a little rectangular mediæval instrument, for example, with one row of keys and no sharps or flats, you can play tunes in the Mixolydian mode with your G drone, in the Aeolian mode by tuning your G drone up a tone to A; in the Ionian mode with your C drone, and in the Dorian mode by tuning your C drone up to D.

If one has the advantage of B flat and F sharp keys, then one has the further possibility of using the modes as set out in numbers 1c, 6c, 4c and 5c.

To decide what mode a tune is in, first write down its lowest and highest notes, mark the final note and check the position of the tones and semitones with the chart. Then transpose it if necessary to a more suitable key. (Example: Slovakian Dance).

Try not to 'modernise' an old tune by altering the notes of the mode or scale with the addition of unsuitable sharps or flats. If you choose the wrong drone you can spoil the melody by creating the wrong harmonies.

Many English, Scottish and Irish melodies are based on a five note (pentatonic) scale, like "The Dear Companion" (page 86). The final note in these should also be the drone note.

On changing key

It is a good thing to have a contrast of keys during a long session of music making, and to relieve the ear of the monotony of a single key, a band of players on non-drone instruments will frequently change to the dominant key (a 5th higher), say from D to A major or from D to the relative minor (B flat), or from C to G major, or from C major to A minor.

Now on the bagpipes or the hurdy-gurdy we cannot do this without changing the drone, though I have heard it done, with horrible results!

What we can do readily and effectively is to change to the tonic minor, i.e. C major to C minor or from G major to G minor. There are plenty of examples of this in 18th century hurdy-gurdy music

SLOVAKIAN DANCE in the Lydian mode

ADDITIONAL REPERTOIRE

CANTIGA DE SANTA MARIA Sempr' acha Santa maria

ST. PAUL'S STEEPLE (in C)

ST. PAUL'S STEEPLE (in G)

MENUET

Op.1 1st Suite. Ch. Baton

PIPER'S FANCY

LAVENDER'S BLUE

LA GIGUE

LA VALSE A CADET

LA BOURRÉE CROISÉE BOURBONNAISE

THE CHOICE OF AN INSTRUMENT

The main types of hurdy-gurdy which are commonly available.

　1. *The organistrum.* This is a large two-person bass instrument suitable for early music groups specialising in the performance of twelfth and thirteenth century music.

　2. *The Box type symphony.* This is the simplest and least expensive hurdy-gurdy to make and the easiest to play since the right hand technique consists solely of turning the handle evenly. The keyboard should be diatonic.

　3. *The 16th century type of symphony* as illustrated by Hieronymous Bosch. This has a diatonic keyboard and a trompette, but could be fitted with a chromatic keyboard. Because of its relatively simple form this is one of the least expensive instruments to make. It is capable of producing a very clear and sweet tone suitable for playing dance music from the sixteenth century or earlier, and also for accompanying the voice.

　4. *17th to 18th centuries.* The type of instrument seen in the picture on page two was the common form during the seventeenth and eighteenth centuries, and was known as the *vielle carrée* or square vielle, though we should nowadays refer to it as trapezoidal. It was the standard French form before 1720, when Charles Baton developed models based on the lute and guitar. Many examples exist in museums, particularly in the Paris Conservatoire collection. It is therefore possible to make exact replicas of these instruments, whereas earlier ones can only be recreated from iconographical evidence.

　5. *The French 18th-19th century vielles.* These have guitar or lute-shaped bodies and finely carved heads. Many of these instruments, notably those of Lambert and the Louvet brothers, are more highly prized for their fine craftsmanship and beautiful tone than the more commonly found examples by Thouvenel and Colson. Their tone is sweeter and quieter than that of later instruments owing to their design and smaller size. Some of them have hardwood soundboards which seem to give a sound more like an oboe. These instruments, or exact copies of them, are the most suitable for the performance of eighteenth century music (see page 68).

　Original instruments are likely to be very expensive and may also be fragile and will need costly repairs. For instance, the soundboard may have to be removed to replace the wheel or its bearings. Any restoration should not be lightly undertaken except by a first-class luthier who is experienced with hurdy-gurdies. It is important to preserve these precious

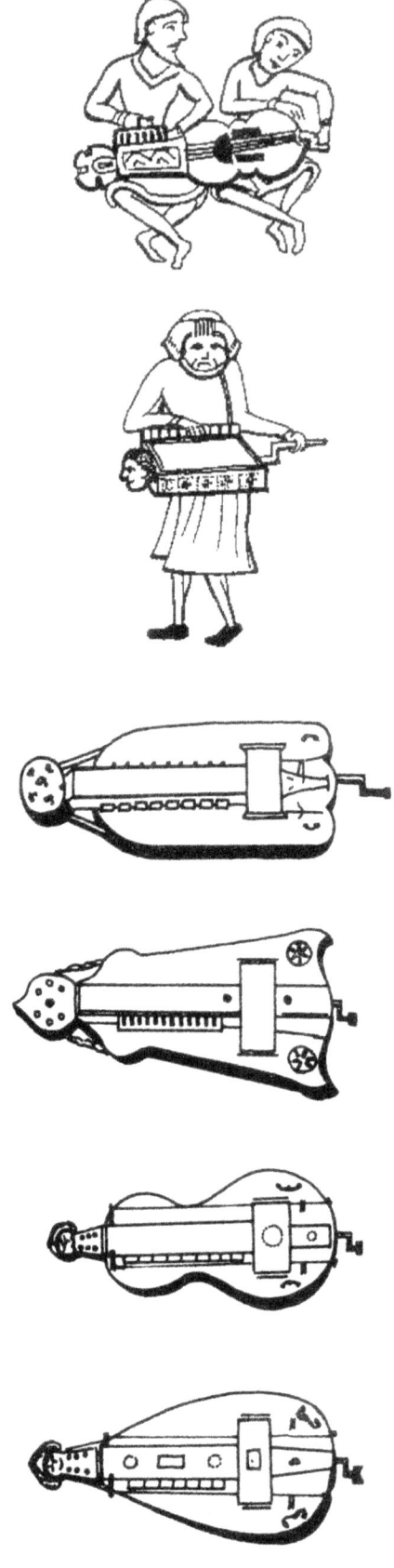

instruments for posterity with as little alteration as possible, because only in this way will knowledge of the old craft techniques survive.

The use of modern materials and techniques, however suitable on new instruments, should be avoided in restoring old ones.

6. Many very fine *nineteenth century French* instruments of the Pajot and Pimpard families exist. These have beautifully painted soundboards and carved heads in the peasant art tradition. The bodies are considerably larger than those of the eighteenth century, with softwood soundboards and wider wheels, giving a loud sound suitable for accompanying outdoor dancing.

7. Good *new instruments* of the above type are still being made by many luthiers in France and by makers in other countries who have studied the French techniques. These instruments produce a loud and resonant tone and are ideally suited for playing dance music. Indeed, they are used in large numbers to accompany the regional folk dances, often along with the cornemuse or cabrette (bagpipes), and frequently out of doors.

It is not possible here to mention all the many types of hurdy-gurdy which makers today are producing, including fine reproductions of German and Flemish 'bauernleier', nor is it possible to say that one kind is better than another. Each has its own character and personality and the choice is wide.

Hurdy-gurdy player. Engraving by Jacques Callot.
17th century

BUYING A HURDY-GURDY

If you are a beginner, buying an instrument for the first time, take a good vielle player with you to try out the instrument.

To test the quality of the axle and bearing first detach the drone strings, lift the chanterelles off the wheel and spin the manivelle. A good wheel should revolve six or seven times with one spin. The axle should be firm and there should be no free play in any direction, as this would cause knocking or rumbling, which you will be able to hear when you replace the strings and turn the wheel fast.

Having tuned the chanterelles, check that the mortises for the keys have been cut in the correct positions. If they are wrong the instrument will be out of tune. Do this by checking the open G with its octave, adjusting the moveable nut if necessary, but keeping the tangents straight (see page 13). Then check that the two C's are in tune, and finally check the other keys for intonation. A badly positioned key means that its tangent will have to be moved too far to the left or right. The keys should be a good fit in their mortises, but should slide without sticking. Don't get powdered resin on the keys. Check that the tangents can be turned for tuning, but are suffiently firm to hold their positions.

The trompette (see page 96). Any deficiency here is not too serious because it is something that you can tackle yourself, but you will need a good vielle player or a maker to advise you.

Some factors which will affect the volume of sound given by a vielle are the diameter of the wheel, the width of the wheel rim, the weight of the strings, the area of the soundboard and the type of wood it is made from, and the depth of the soundbox.

The real test is in the playing. Be wary of buying an instrument from a maker who cannot demonstrate that the instrument works well. The best makers keep their instruments for several weeks before selling, allowing them to settle down and final adjustments to be made.

A good hurdy-gurdy should sound beautiful and feel alive and rewarding to play. Remember that the chanterelle tone is very much affected by the way the cotton and resin are applied.

There are now several English makers who are producing good hurdy-gurdies, and there are many more in France, Germany, America and other countries.

MAKING A HURDY-GURDY

In making such a complicated instrument as the hurdy-gurdy there are many pitfalls for the unwary beginner. You would be well advised not to try to be too independent, but to learn as much as possible from the best makers and their instruments. If you are in touch with someone who already has a good instrument your task will be that much easier.

It is important to copy a tried design and to work from a reliable set of plans. Unfortunately, there are a few makers who sell hurdy-gurdies which they have made from insufficiently detailed drawings, and without understanding the basic principles of the design and regulation of the instrument. Their clients, thinking they have got a bargain, find to their dismay that the instrument gives them no joy, but only endless trouble.

If you make instruments to sell, have them thoroughly tested by a good player before putting them on the market.

PLANS

Plans for making various models of hurdy-gurdy are available from Muskett Music by email: michael@muskett-music.co.uk.

Chris Eaton, hurdy-gurdy maker

HOW TO TRUE THE WHEEL

Strap the instrument on as if you are going to play it and slacken the drone strings. Place on the soundboard a thin piece of cardboard cut out like a template to fit close up to the wheel on each side in order to protect the soundboard from being scratched. Using a sharp blade, such as a chisel or plane blade, hold the cutting edge against the wheel, supported on the card, and turn the wheel briskly, removing very fine shavings until all irregularities have disappeared. Don't do this very often, or the wheel will become too small! The edge of the wheel should be flat and the string pressure should be fractionally less on the keybox side than it is on the bridge side. Finish by applying powdered resin on a cloth, and rubbing it into the grain of the wood by turning the wheel. Excess resin may be removed with a clean cork.

N.B. This procedure should only be undertaken by a good instrument maker who is thoroughly familiar with the hurdy-gurdy.

THE MOST COMMON FAULTS AND THEIR CAUSES	
Rumbling or knocking.	Loose wheel bearings
Regular pulsation or fluctuation of pitch on each turn of the wheel.	The wheel is not circular.
Cotton wool will not wind on evenly, or wears unevenly.	The wheel rim is not flat, or is not angled parallel to the strings. The strings should touch the full width of the wheel rim.
Pitch of chanterelle leaps up an octave, particularly when turning the wheel quickly.	Insufficient pressure on the wheel, or not enough rosin.
Harsh grating tone, with chanterelles being pulled in the direction of the wheel turn.	Too much pressure on the wheel, or too much rosin.
Upper notes unstable or out of tune.	Too much cotton wool or uneven cotton wool.
Rattling, buzzing or vibration on one note.	a) Tangent loose b) Tangents out of tune c) The two tangents are not touching the strings simultaneously.

HOW TO MAKE AND ADJUST THE TROMPETTE

The Function of the *Trompette*

The *trompette* enables the player to articulate some or all of the notes of the melody by means of a buzzing tone which emanates from the little loose bridge or *chien* (dog), over which the *trompette* string passes. (Fig.1)

Fig. 1 The trompette bridge

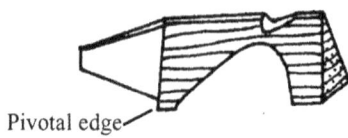

Pivotal edge

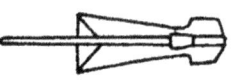

from above

The Action of the *Trompette*

Whereas all the other bridges provide a firm support for the strings, this *chien* is finely adjusted to be in a state of equilibrium such that the smallest acceleration above the normal speed of the rotating wheel will set it into a rapid trembling or vibration. The pointed end, or tenon, of the *chien* fits into a mortise cut into the drone bridge. The *chien* moves like a pivoting hammer, beating on the soundboard. A thin plate of ivory is sometimes inlaid in order to prevent the soundboard from wearing.

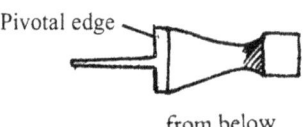

from below

Making and Adjusting the *Chien*

1. Set up the *trompette* string so that it forms a straight line between the *oreille* (ear), the wheel and the point of attachment at the edge of the soundboard. The string must be parallel to the rim of the wheel, and must not press too hard against it.

2. The height of the *chien* should be 10-12 mm, and must be the same height as the notch on the *oreille*, so that the string lies parallel to the soundboard between the *oreille* and the *chien*. (Fig. 2)

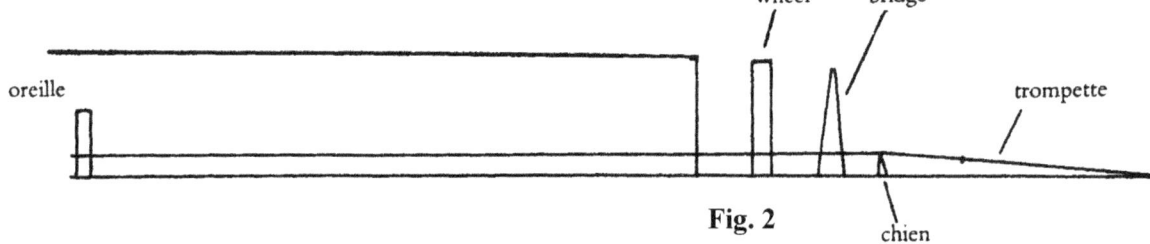

Fig. 2

3. The length of the *chien* can be determined by measuring the distance between the drone bridge and the string (B-C), adding the length of the mortise in the bridge (A-B) - about 8mm - and then adding 7-8mm for the 'foot' (D-E). The total length will be about 30-35mm. (Figs. 3 and 4).

4. The *chien* is usually cut from well-seasoned hard maple with the grain running parallel to the foot. Cut the tenon so that it fits well into the mortise, without any lateral play, but pivots up and down without friction. The mortise should be kept free of dust and resin.

5. Slip the half-made *chien* into the mortise and under the *trompette* string and cut a notch at the point where the string rests on it.

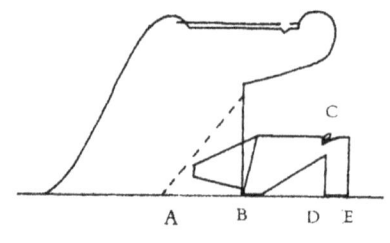

Fig. 3

6. Cut the inner edge of the 'foot' upwards directly below the notch and shape the underside of the *chien* so that it has a narrow pivoting surface or 'hinge' at A and a wider-based 'foot' B. (Fig.5).

7. One must ensure that these two surfaces (A and B, Fig. 5) sit absolutely level on the soundboard. With the string and the *chien* in position, slip a piece of fine sandpaper under the *chien*, and pressing gently downwards, withdraw it, repeating the action several times.

8. Fasten an adjusting cord of thin gut (about 0.5mm diameter) round the *trompette* string with a special loop (Fig. 6) and attach it to the peg in the tail-piece. The loop must allow the string to slide freely through it so that the cord can be pushed nearer to or further from, the *chien*. The cord must be parallel to the sound-board. As the peg is turned it will pull the *trompette* string towards the tail-piece, but the angle here must not be too great (Fig.7).

9. The last two adjustments are used to regulate the sensitivity of the *chien*. Without any tightening of the peg the *trompette* will sound like a normal drone string. As you turn the peg with the left hand while turning the manivelle steadily with the right hand, the *chien* will start to vibrate. The buzz should sound only at the beginning of each stroke and should be silent during the remaining turn of the wheel.

Note: Take care that you do not screw the end of the adjusting peg down onto the soundboard.

The following factors affect the tone and sensitivity of the *chien*:

a) The dimensions of the base of the 'foot'.
b) The position of the notch. Cut this rather far back initially, and gradually cut it closer to the tenon until you get the right response.
c) The overall weight of the *chien*.
d) Distance from bridge to *chien* foot.
e) Height of *chien*.
f) The fit of the tenon in the mortise.
g) The angle of the hinge or pivot and the accuracy with which it is cut.
h) The distance from the bridge to the chien. This should be one third of the distance from the bridge to the tirant.

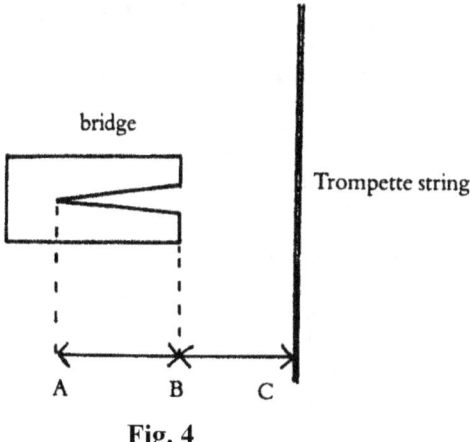

Fig. 4

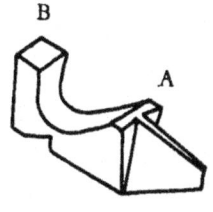

Fig. 5

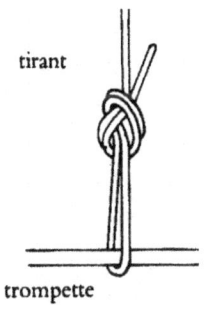

Fig. 6

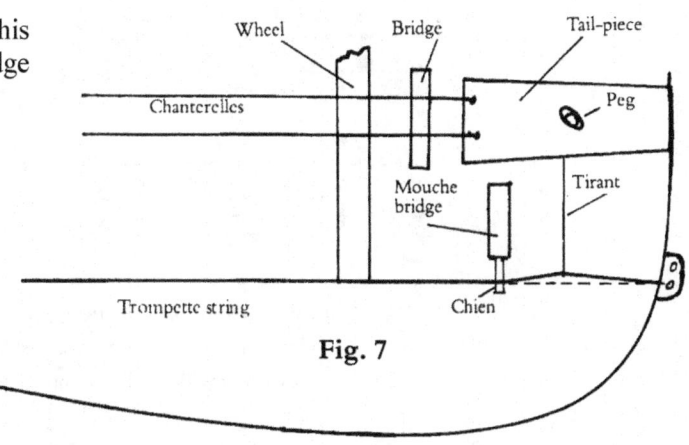

Fig. 7

FRENCH-ENGLISH GLOSSARY

l'âme—soundpost
l'axe—axle, crank shaft
la boîte—box
le boîtier—case
le bourdon—drone
le bouton—button
le boyau—gut
la cache-roue—wheel cover
la caisse—body, soundbox
la chanterelle—melody string
la charnière—hinge
le chevalet—bridge
la cheville—peg
le chien—dog
le clavier—keyboard or keybox
la colophane—resin
la corde—string
le cordier—tail-piece
le coton—cotton-wool
le coup de poignet—flick of the wrist
la courroie—strap
le couvercle—lid
le détaché—separation, staccato, articulation
l'éclisse—rib of soundbox
l'encoche—notch

la feutre—felt
le fond—back
gros—big
la manivelle—crank
mobile—moveable
la mouche—fly
les oreilles— 'ear' bridges
l'ouie—sound holes
le petit bourdon—small drone
la poignée—handle, knob
le poignet—wrist
la roue—wheel
les sautereaux—tangents
le sillet—nut (moveable)
la table d'harmonie—soundboard, belly, top
les timbres de résonance—sympathetic strings
le tirant—adjusting cord
la touche—key
tourne à gauche—tuning key (lit. turn to the left)
la trompette—trumpet
le trou de graissage—oil hole
la vielle à roue—hurdy-gurdy
le vielleux/la vielleuse—hurdy-gurdy player

Cotillon from *Pièces Choisies* published by Ballard in Paris in 1732. Most vielle music in the first half of the eighteenth century was written with the G clef on the first line of the stave.

18th CENTURY MUSIC FOR THE HURDY-GURDY

There is a great deal of original unpublished music for hurdy-gurdy solo, for two hurdy-gurdies or musettes, hurdy-gurdy with figured bass accompaniment, sonatas, suites, concertos, etc. Original copies are held by the British Library, London, the Bibliotheque Nationale, Paris and other sources and is available on microfilm. Many examples are given in Marianne Bröcker's 'Die Drehleier' and in 'Shepherds' Delight' by J. Ralyea. Here follows a short list of works which I have come across. Those which have been republished in recent times, some edited as recorder pieces, are given with the publishers' names.

Baton, Charles Six Sonatas pour la vielle. Op. 3   Les Amusements d'une Heure. Duos pour la vièlle. Op. 4.

Boismortier. Joseph Bodin de Six Suites for two musettes or vielles. Op. XV11 (1727) Hortus Musicus No. 206. Bärenreiter.

Boismortier, J. B. de First and Second Suites for hurdy-gurdy duo. Op. 11 Editions Fuzeau. Editions Fuzeau publishes a number of 18th century works originally for the hurdy-gurdy.

Buterne, Charles Six Sonates pour la vielle. Op.2 Four with bass continuo and two en duo.

Chédeville l'Ainé Six sonatilles galantes for musettes or vielles with bass cont. Op. 6. Otto Heinrich Noetzel Verlag

Chédeville, Nicholas
Suite, 'La President' (arr. for recorder and harpsichord by C. Dolmetsch) Schott and Co. Six Suites for two melody instruments by Boismortier, Chédeville, deLavigne. Augener, London

Chédeville, Esprit Philippe Six Galante Duos. Hortus Musicus No. 199

Chédeville le Jeune Amusements Champêtres. Book 1. Suite No. 1. For hurdy-gurdy duo. Muskett Music

Chédeville, Nicolas 'Le Printemps ou les saisons amusantes'. (Concerto by Vivaldi, the Four Seasons, arranged for musette or vielle, with violins, flute and bass.)

Corrette, Gaston. Pièces de Fun for hurdy-gurdy duo. Muskett Music

Corrette, Michel. Trois Concertos de Berger Fortuné, for musette, vielle, violon, flute, recorder, oboe and basso cont.

de Lavigne, Philibert
Six Suites for two musettes or vielles. Op. 1 (1731)
Six Sonatas for musette or vielle with bass continuo. Op. 2. Otto Heinrich Noetzel Verlag.
Les Fleurs. Pieces for musettes or vielles accompanied by violin or flute. Op.4 Amadeus Verlag.

Haydn, Joseph
Five concertos for lira organizzate, two violins, two violas, 'cello and two horns. Hob. V11 1-5
Eight Notturni for two lira organizzate, two violins or clarinets, two violas, 'cello and two horns.
These works were written by Haydn about 1785 for Ferdinand IV, King of Naples and Sicily, for the lira organizzate, a kind of hurdy-gurdy combined with an organ. These are published by Doblinger Verlag, Vienna, and are available in score, parts or as a piano reduction.

Mozart, Leopold
The Peasants' Wedding (1755) for 2 horns, 2 oboes, violins, leier (hurdy-gurdy) dudelsack (bagpipes), viola, bassoon and violoncelli. K.V. 601 No. 2.

Mozart, Wolfgang Amadeus
Four German Dances for 2 violins, bass, 2 flutes, 2 oboes, 2 bassoons, leier, 2 horns, 2 clarinen und pauken. K.V. 601 No. 3.

Naudot
Babioles for two vielles, musettes, etc. c. 1730. Edition Schott 5734 (RMS 2028).

Vivaldi, Antonio (Attrib.) Il Pastor Fido. Six Sonatas for musette, vielle, etc. and bass cont. Op. 13. These sonatas are actually by N. Chédeville and other Parisian composers, who published them under Vivaldi's name. Hortus Musicus No. 135. Bärenreiter.

M.Fromenteau and G. Casteuble (Editors) *Duets for the hurdy-gurdy* 25 pieces by 18th century French composers for two hurdy-gurdies tuned to C. Text in French and English. Editions J. M. Fuzeau.

BIBLIOGRAPHY

Bachman, Werner. The Origins of Bowing. Oxford (1969)

Baines, Francis. Introducing the Hurdy-gurdy. Early Music Quarterly. OUP (January 1975)

Bonnaud, Louis. A la rechérche des plus anciennes vielles à roue. Folklore de France. No. 150

Boulesteix, Jean-Louis. Memoire de la Vielle. CDRP de Limoges. 23 Avenue Alexis Carrel. 87036 Limoges CEDEX. France. 1982

Marcello Bono. La Ghironda. Arnoldo Forni Editore, Bologna, Italy (1989)

Bröcker, Marianne. Die Drehleier. Ihr Bau und ihre Geschichte. Verlag für systematische Musikwissenschaft. Bonn-Bad Godesburg. (A detailed and comprehensive study in two volumes.) 1977

Buchner, Alexander. Musical Instruments—An Illustrated History. Octopus.

Chassaing, J-F. La Vielle et les Luthiers de Jenzat. Aux Amoureux de Science, Combronde. 1987. ISBN 2-905543-12-4.

Galpin, Canon F.W. Old English Instruments of Music. Methuen. 1965

Green, Robert. The Hurdy-gurdy in Eighteenth Century France. Indiana University Press.1995 ISBN 0-253-20942-0

Hollinger, Roland. Les Musiques à Bourdons. Vielles a roue et cornemuses. La Flute de Pan, 55 rue de Rome, Paris. 1982

Imbert, Pierre. and **Rouger, J.** Editors. Vielle à Roue, Territoires illimités.1996, ISBN 2.910432-06-8, FAMDT. Saint-Jouin-de-Milly, France. (French with English abstracts)

Kunz, Ludvik. Die Volksinstrumente der Tschechoslowakei. Teil 1. VEB Deutsche Verlag Musik, Leipzig 1974

Leppert, Richard. Arcadia at Versailles: Noble Amateur Musicians and their musettes and hurdy-gurdies at the French Court. A Visual Study. Swets & Zeitlinger B.V. Amsterdam and Lisse.1978. ISBN 90-265-0246X

Montague, Jeremy. The World of Mediæval and Renaissance Instruments. David and Charles, 1978.

Page, Christopher. The Mediæval Organistrum and Sinfonia, Galpin Society Journal No. XXXIV

Palmer, Susann & S. The Hurdy-gurdy. David and Charles, 1980. ISBN0 7153 7888 0

Panum, Hortense. Stringed Instruments of the Middle Ages. Reeves.1971.

Ralyea, John. Shepherd's Delight. Guide to the 18th century repertoire for hurdy-gurdy, musette, etc. 1981 The Hurdy-gurdy Press, 5309. S. Ellis, Chicago, Ill. 60615.

Rault, Christian. L'Organistrum. Les origines de la vielle a roue. Aux Amateurs de Livres, 62 Avenue de Suffren, Paris. 1985. ISBN 2.905053.12-7

Sarosi, Balint. Die Volkinstrumente Ungarns. VEB Deutsche Verlag Musik, Leipzig 1974

Winternitz, Emanuel. Musical Instruments and their Symbolism in Western Art. Faber. 1967

Organistrum and psaltery players
From a German miniature (c.1360)

METHODS

18th century

Ballard, J.B. Christophe. Pièces Choisies pour la Vielle, a l'usage des commencants, avec des instructions pour toucher, et pour entretenir cet instrument. Paris (1732)

Bordet. Méthode Raisonée pour apprendre la musique d'une facon plus clair (1755)

Dupuit, Baptiste. Principes pour Toucher de la vielle, Avec Six Sonates pour cet Instrument, qui conviennent aux violon, flute, clavessin, etc. Oeuvre 1er. Paris (1741)

Bouin, Francois. La Vielleuse Habile, ou Nouvelle Méthode, Courte, très facile, et très sure, Pour Apprendre a jouer de la Vielle. Ouvre III. Paris (1761)
La Vielleuse Habile. Éditions Minkoff, Geneva ISBN 2-8266-0815-0.

Corrette, Michel. La Belle Vielleuse. Méthode pour apprendre facilement à jouer de la vielle, contenant des leçons etc... Avec des Jolis Airs et Ariettes en duo, deux suites avec la Basse et des Chansons, par Mr Corrette. Paris 1783 (Bibl. De Rouen).

La Belle Vielleuse (Facsimile edition of the above). Introduction de Claude Flagel. Musiciens et musique en Normandy. Supplément. Flagel's introduction is a valuable comparative study of the musical examples used by other composers of the 18th century, including Hotterre, Chédeville, Bouin and Dupuit.

Méthode pour apprendre à jouer de la vielle par Corrette. Costallat et Cie. (British Library) (This appears to be a nineteenth century edition, with numerous mistakes and omissions and without duos, bass parts or songs.)

20th century

* **Heintzen, J-F.** Pratique de jeu de vielle Centre-France. Relevè de notes - conseils et exercises pour vielles en rè. 1995. AMTA, Riom, France.

* **Rivière, Gaston**. Méthode de vielle. 24 rue d'Alembert, 01300 Montlucon, France.

* **Dubois, André**. Méthode de Vielle en 12 leçons. Chavignol, 183000 Sancerre, France.
This includes a 45 rpm disc illustrating each lesson.

* **Frankfurt Hurdy-gurdy Ensemble, Die Hummel**. Die Drehleier: Handhabung und Spieltechnik. Musik-Glier KG, Allerheiligenstrasse 17, D-6000. Frankfurt 1. Germany.

These methods are for hurdy-gurdy tuned in D. All the others for hurdy-gurdy tuned in C.

Making and maintenance

Buchanan, G. The Making of Stringed Instruments. A Workshop Guide.Batsford 1989 030 0 7134 5643 C

Coates, K. Geometry & Proportion in the Art of Lutherie. Clarendon Press 1985 0 30 019 816246 4

Destrem, P. & Heidemann, V. The Hurdy-gurdy: Adjustment and Maintenance. AMTA. 193.
ISBN 2-9507682-0-2 (In German, French and English.)

Fettweis, J. De la manière d'entretenir la vielle. 1978. 80, Tiège, B 4883 SART, Belgium.

Tolley, B. Making Musical Instruments. (Contains a chapter on making a simple hurdy-gurdy as a school project). Wayland Publishers, England. 1978

Dewit, H. & Moonan, T. Draailierboek. Vereniging voor Huismuziek. Holland. 1982-1985?

Interpretation

Brown. H.M. Embellishing Sixteenth-century Music. Oxford University Press. 1976. ISBN 0 19 3231751

Couperin. F. The Art of Playing the Harpsichord. Ed. Margery Halford. Alfred Publishing Co. 1974

Donington, R. A Performer's Guide to Baroque Music. Faber. 1973. ISBN 0 571 09797 9

Veilhan, J-C. The Rules of Musical Interpretation in the Baroque Era (17th-18th centuries)
A. Leduc. Paris. 1977. ISBN 2 85689 008 3 (Also available in French.)

INDEX OF PIECES

England, Scotland and Ireland

Auld lang syne	88
The Black Nag	86
Bobby Shaftoe	38
Canon by Thomas Tallis	35
The Chestnut tree	35
The Dear Companion	86
Drink to me only	40
Davy Knick-knack	91
Goddesses	86
Go tell Aunt Rhodie (American)	38
Haste to the Wedding—Irish jig	86
Jenny Pluck Pears—Playford, 17th C.	56
Jingle Bells	88
The Keel Row	54
Lavender's Blue	85
Lilliburlero—Irish. 17th C.	53
The Miller of Dee	54
Nobody's Jig	62
Piper's Fancy	85
Robin Hood and the Pedlar	82
Nonesuch	87
Scarborough Fair	41
Simple Gifts, American Shaker melody	38
St. Paul's Steeple C & G	84

France
Traditional

L'Ageasse	47
Au Clair de la Lune	25
Auprès de ma Blonde	52
La Bourrée Croisée Bourbonnaise	89
La Bourrée des Dindes	45
La Bourrée de Lascroux	49
La Bourrée de Morvan	51
Bourrée Valse	51
La Bourrée Villebret	46
La Chèvre	45
La Crousada de Saint-Martinien	90
La Gigue	89
La Granda Aiga (Valsa)	67
Jean Danse Mieux que Pierre	62
La Marche de Brive	90
Marche: Perquei me fasetz-vous la mina	90
Mazurka	59
La Montagnarde	46
Les Moutons	45
Le Pas d'Eté	50
Le Pas des Moissonneurs	51
La Pépue	48
La pluie, le vent	28
La Polka du Pée Faulon	39
La Polka Piquée	49
Savez-vous planter les Choux?	37

Scottish	50
Scottish-Valse	58
Tres Cacaus	91
La Valse a Cadet	89
Valse à Eric	51
La Varsovienne	91
Le Vieille Scottish	58
Vendôme	25

France
16th and 18th century

Ah! Vous dirai-je, maman	87
Les Bergeries (Fr. Couperin, arr. *Bouin*)	74
Les Bouffons (The Buffoon's Dance) *Arbeau*	37
Le Branle du Coq (duet) *Chédeville*	50
Le Branle des Chevaux, *Arbeau*	87
Cher Silvandre (duo) *Chédeville*	63
Cotillon 'J'ai du bon tabac'	48
Fanfare, *Bouin*	87
Fanfare (duo) *Chédeville*	54
La jeune Isabelle, *Chédeville*	65
March from the Peasants' Wedding. *L. Mozart*	61
Marlbourg (duet) arr. *Corrette*	88
Marmotte	56
First Menuet, *Bouin*	43
Second Menuet, *Bouin*	61
Menuet (duo) *Bâton* 85	
Le Mirliton, *Chédeville l'Aîné*	45
Musette (duo) *Bertin*	75
Noël, Joseph est bien marié	65
Four Preludes, *Bouin*	70
Ou son donc ces amants?	63
Quittez Pasteurs (Les Pistolets)	38
Reveillez vous	40
Rigaudon (duo) *Boismortier*	76
Rondeau (duet) *Chédeville l'Aîné*	47
Tes beaux yeux	41
Vaudeville	37

Other Countries

Hungarian tune	91
Kiekbusch	39
Slovakian dance	83
Die Rommelpot (Flemish)	65
Yag har vatti Höja (Swedish)	62

Mediæval

Chanson de Mai, *Moniot d'Arras*, 13th cent.	80
Cantiga de Santa Maria (Spain) 13th cent.	84
Ductia, 13th cent.	80
Joliveté et bone amours, *Jehan d'Esquiri*, 13th cent.	43
Lamento di Tristano, *Anon*, 14th cent.	81
Quand je voy hiver retorner, *Colin Muset*, 13th cent.	80

LIST OF ILLUSTRATIONS

Photograph of Doreen Muskett	iv
The Hurdy-gurdy Player. Oil painting by Georges de la Tour (c.1630)	2
Portico de la Gloria (c.1188). Cathedral of Santiago de Compostela	3
Miniature from the Luttrell Psalter (c.1330)	4
Old Sarah, the hurdy-gurdy player. From Mayhew's 'London Labour and the London Poor' (1851)	5
Shepherd and shepherdess, porcelain figures. Collection Michelle Fromenteau	5
'Fanchon la Vielleuse', heroine of many popular plays, ballets and operas in the 18th and 19th centuries	6
Members of the folklore group, l'Eicolo dau Barbichet (Limoges)	6
The Hungarian hurdy-gurdy player, Robert Mandel	7
Tourne-à-gauche or wooden tuning key	11
Technical illustration showing the working parts of the hurdy-gurdy Marin Mersenne (1636)	13
Putting cotton on the chanterelle	14
Correct sitting position for playing the hurdy-gurdy	15
The French hurdy-gurdy player, Gaston Rivière	16
The right hand holding the manivelle	17
The right hand showing the position of the knob (poignée)	17
Position of the left hand on the keybox	17
From the Encyclopédie of Diderot and d'Alembert, Paris (1767)	19
Organistrum players. Miniature from the Hunterian Psalter (12th cent.)	25
Correct position of the wrist	30
Faulty position of the wrist	30
Vielle Player from the Auvergne adjusting his trompette while entertaining passers-by in the Place du Trocadero, Paris	32
Nigel Eaton	32
Fish following a boat, attracted by the sound of a symphony From a miniature in an English Bestiary (14th cent.)	39
Departure of the little Savoyards (19th cent.)	57
St. Chartier hurdy-gurdy dance group	59
A Hungarian hurdy-gurdy	61
A lady playing her vielle. 18th century painting	68
Title page of a set of suites for two musettes or vielles by Chédeville le Jeune	69
Design from a gingerbread mould. Bagpiper and hurdy-gurdy player. Slovakia (18th cent.)	76
Detail of box-symphony showing keys with two positions for some tangents.	78
Playing a realisation of the organistrum of Santiago de Compostela, with the keybox cover slid back to show the tangents	78
Miniature from the Cantigas de Santa Maria (13th cent.)	79
A mediæval minstrel arrives to entertain a noble lord at his table French miniature of the Romance of Girart de Nevers	81
The main types of hurdy-gurdy	92
Hurdy-gurdy player by Callot	93
Chris Eaton, hurdy-gurdy maker	94
Cotillon from Pieces Choisies published by Ballard. Paris (1732)	98
Organistrum and psaltery. from a German miniature (c. 1360)	100
Dwarf hurdy-gurdy player by Callot	104

www.ingramcontent.com/pod-product-compliance
Lightning Source LLC
Chambersburg PA
CBHW081437300426
44108CB00017BA/2390